More Acclaim for *Educating with Aloha*

"What a gift this book is to our communities as we rethink what education could be for our students! As a pioneer in the field, Jan teaches us through her highlighted collection of blogs. Come share the wisdom of a pioneer whose reflections help us imagine a new and better future for all."

—Cris Waldfogel, Director for Professional Learning and Leadership, PBL Works

"Once again, Jan Iwase shares with us much to reflect on and learn from. As a school leader, Jan possessed a clear, strong vision and stayed true to her core values, both of which remain relevant to the challenges we face today. From embedding aloha into her school culture to using social media as a means to connect and learn with others, Jan serves as a model for thoughtful educators who aspire to lead and not merely survive our current crisis, but to thrive."

—Derek Minakami, principal, National Board Certified Teacher, Hawai'i Department of Education

"In *Educating with Aloha* Jan focuses on the essential balance required in education. The three Rs are still relevant today, but what about the five Cs? Jan's writing makes me reflect on my own journey from my sometimes "tumbly" youth to now as a superintendent. Her forty-five-year journey through education is an amazing example of how we need to continually grow and change to meet the needs of our *keiki*. COVID-19 has changed our world, and Jan highlights the many ways we can take what we've learned and use it to make education—and the world—a better place."

—Chad Keone Farias, Complex Area Superintendent, Hawai'i Department of Education

"For a very long time, since the beginning of our current model of education in 1893, if we heard from public school principals at all, it was about how to manage schools and close the so-called achievement gap. Rarely did we hear from imaginative, creative and innovative principals dancing on the edge of what school could be, as the world entered its current technological age of information and acceleration. Equally rare was the principal who made the inner workings of her mind and heart accessible to parents and community members through mediums like blogs. Retired Hawai'i public school principal Jan Iwase proves the remarkable exception. In *Educating With Aloha* she provides both a historical window into those blogs and into her own growth as a leader on an inspiring journey of learning. Jan's book should be required reading for education leadership programs across the nation."

—Josh Reppun, podcast host of *What School Could Be in Hawai'i* and film producer and co-director of *The Innovation Playlist*

Educating with Aloha

Reflections from the Heart on Teaching and Learning

With warmest aloha,
Jan Iwase
May 2022

Educating with Al♥ha

Reflections from the Heart on Teaching and Learning

Jan Iwase

LEGACY ISLE
PUBLISHING

This book is dedicated to my parents, Keiji and Vivian Amemiya, who instilled in me a lifetime love for learning and encouraged me to pursue my dreams.

© 2021 Jan Iwase

All rights reserved. No part of this book may be reproduced in any form or by any electronic or mechanical means, including information retrieval systems, without prior written permission from the publisher, except for brief passages quoted in reviews.

ISBN 978-1-948011-57-0

Library of Congress Control Number: 2021911006

A portion of the proceeds from sales of this book support the National Kidney Foundation of Hawai`i.

Design and production
Ingrid Lynch

Front cover illustrations iStock/izumikobayashi, background iStock/jammydesign

Legacy Isle Publishing
1000 Bishop St., Ste. 806
Honolulu, HI 96813
Toll-free 1-866-900-BOOK
info@legacyislepublishing.net
www.legacyislepublishing.net

10 9 8 7 6 5 4 3 2 1

Printed in Korea

Contents

	Foreword by Justin Iwase	13
	Introduction	17
1	A Culture of Aloha	21
2	Positive Relationships with Our Students	41
3	Explore, Discover, Create, and Share	64
4	Build Teacher Capacity	99
5	Partnering with Families and the Community	125
6	What Does the Future Hold for Education?	146
	Afterword	171
	References	173

Acknowledgments

Writing a book takes time and effort as well as the support and guidance from many individuals, and I would like to acknowledge these special people.

- First, to my husband, **Randy**, who challenged me by asking tough questions about my "why?" for writing this book. If you know Randy, you know he doesn't mince words, but I know he was pushing me to be better. When he read my final manuscript and stated that as a non-educator, he enjoyed it and learned a lot, I felt gratified.
- To our oldest son, **Justin**—Thank you for reading my manuscript and for writing such a meaningful foreword. You were always a great son and big brother, and now you are an awesome dad to Jace and Jayden. We are proud of you.
- To our middle son, **Jarand**—We miss you. Not a day goes by that Dad and I don't think about you. Know that you are always in our hearts and in our thoughts.
- To our youngest son, **Jordan**—You took a different path from your brothers by serving in the Air Force for six years before completing your college degree. I marvel at how much you've grown and learned from your experiences.
- To **Mom** and my siblings, **Corinne**, **Debbie**, **Roy**, and **Chris**—I was so fortunate to grow up in our family. Thank you for always being so supportive of me.
- To our **HKES/DKIES ʻohana**, the staff, students, families, and school community—For 15 years we were family, and

our school was my second home, a place I loved. *Mahalo* for all the memories.
- To **Ted Dintersmith, Cris Waldfogel, Derek Minakami, Peter DeWitt, Chad Keone Farias**, and **Josh Reppun**—Mahalo for reading my manuscript and writing a testimonial for my book. You are all such busy people, but you made the time to help me out. Your support means so much to me.
- To **Tami Sego, Dimpna Figuracion, Jonathon Medeiros, Michelle Lau, Yuuko Arikawa-Cross**, and **Kristi Higuchi-Delos Santos**—Thank you for reading earlier drafts of my book. I value your feedback and support; it made a difference in my final manuscript.
- To **Kat Araujo, Carol Conway, Jennifer Eugenio, Peter DeWitt, Eric Sheninger, George Couros, Michelle Colte, Dr. Julia Myers**, and **Dr. Richard Jones**—Thank you for giving me permission to include your stories and experiences in my book; it would not be the same without that personal touch.
- To **George Engebretson** and the staff at Legacy Isle Publishing—I couldn't have done this alone. I appreciate your professionalism and your support.
- Most of all, thank you to all of you for reading my book. I hope it will inspire you to make a difference for our students.

Foreword

by Justin Iwase

When I was younger, I always saw my mother as an incredible educator of students, but as I've grown older, I've realized her real strength is as a student of education. Even in retirement, she is constantly striving to better herself—both through learning and teaching others. This book is a testament to her lifelong passion.

Mom always found opportunities to teach my brothers and me and used methods that were captivating and fun. I wasn't always the best "school" student—I have a penchant for procrastination—but Mom always managed to keep our attention. We'd bring home caterpillars and watch them go through metamorphosis. We'd learn about light refracting through prisms, magnetic poles, or create tornadoes using water bottles. No opportunity was ever wasted.

Looking back, I realize how blessed I was to have an educator as a mother. I've always been curious—I owe that to Mom for always forcing me to look at the world in a multitude of ways. She'd come home with problems for us to solve and ask how we got the answer. She encouraged us to find alternate solutions to problems. With Mom, it wasn't always about memorizing things—she wanted us to learn the processes, because she understood that the method was more important than the answer. After seeing the evolution of education, I realize that she was ahead of her time.

When my two sons started going to school, I had discussions with Mom about how much education had changed since I was in elementary school. She explained to me in detail about group learning and how the answer was secondary to understanding the solution. I realized how much work she had put into learning how to teach—it was eye-opening for me. She was a woman with many years of teaching experience, still trying to be the best possible educator and leader. She had taught us to always strive for greatness, and was leading by example.

Two years ago, after her retirement, Mom made plans to take us on a well-earned family vacation. This was not something we were able to do when I was younger, as my brothers and I were always busy with sports and Dad was in politics. We decided on a Revolutionary/Civil War tour—Boston, Philadelphia, Washington, DC, and ending in Orlando and Disney World. My two sons were at an age where we felt like they could appreciate a "learning vacation," since we were visiting the birthplace of our country. In true "mom fashion" she planned to have my sons blog about their experiences every night.

The trip was incredible. We visited the Kennedy Museum, walked the Freedom Trail, toured Gettysburg, saw the graves of our Founding Fathers, toured the Capitol, and visited various Smithsonian museums. But the blog was a failure. Mom had failed to consider exhaustion at the end of every night combined with the inattentiveness of a nine-year-old and a 12-year-old on vacation. Mom, always patient and always willing to adapt, immediately recognized this, and opted to just let the boys enjoy the vacation and absorb the information. It worked—the boys still look back fondly on that vacation and recall numerous events from those two weeks. Mom, in all her wisdom, knew that sometimes the best way to learn is to just step back and allow learning to occur.

It was no surprise to me when Mom, fresh off retirement, decided to write a book about her experiences—she had never been one to remain idle. She had already started a blog while a principal at Daniel K. Inouye Elementary School and was continually updating it, so this was an obvious transition. *Leading with Aloha: From the Pineapple Fields to the Principal's Office* was the perfect title for her book—everything Mom did while teaching was done with kindness, empathy, and persistence.

Mom knows that "Leading with Aloha" and "Educating with Aloha" cannot just be catchphrases—they must be lifestyles. Teaching people is hard, and leading leaders is harder. To do so with wisdom and grace without being overbearing is an art, and Mom has mastered it. She knows how to bring out the best in people and how to use people's strengths to make a group collectively better. Her long-term success as both a teacher and as a principal is working proof of her methods.

A Native American proverb reads, "We do not inherit the earth from our ancestors—we borrow it from our children." Everyone in Mom's life—her students, her teachers, and her family—have all been beneficiaries of her embracing this philosophy. Whether you are an educator or not, we are all teachers in some way, and reading Mom's books will provide a unique insight that adds value to your own teaching methods. Mom has been the greatest teacher in my life and an inspiration to me. I hope you find as much pleasure reading this book as I have.

Introduction

My first book, *Leading with Aloha: From the Pineapple Fields to the Principal's Office*, was published in 2019, and I was often asked when I would write a second book. Frankly, I had not given it any thought, but when COVID-19 hit, I found myself with time on my hands, time to think and reflect. As a retired educator, one of my major concerns was how this pandemic would impact our students, teachers, school leaders, and schools in general. This is the perfect time to discuss how to make schools more relevant in this, the 21st century.

It took a pandemic for schools to realize the need to change how we teach and how students learn. Transitioning from in-person, face-to-face, scheduled classes to virtual or distance learning was a huge learning curve for many educators and their students. In the process, educators and communities realized the urgency to ask difficult questions: How can we create a school system that addresses the needs of different kinds of learners, especially those who do not learn in the traditional way? Do we want students to memorize facts and procedures so they can pass a test, or do we want their curiosity and passions to drive what and how they learn and apply new information? How do we address the inequality and inequity in public education here in our country, which is a reflection of our society? How can we resolve the teacher shortage problem, especially now, when many have left or are planning to leave the profession? How can we make schools more relevant? There are so many questions related to education that we should be discussing. If we truly agree that our children deserve a public education system that will prepare them to be the leaders of tomorrow, then let's work together to ensure that our schools are a priority.

Staying home and reading and reacting to articles, blogs, or tweets on social media made me realize that I was ready to write another book, one which would be geared to those who are invested in education, not just teachers and school leaders, but parents and community members as well. I already had a foundation—my blog—which I started back in 2012. This blog became an important vehicle for me to share my thoughts, my opinions, my hopes, and my experiences as an educator. I also share personal stories and global and leadership issues via this blog. I reviewed all of my nearly 300 blog posts and selected the ones that I thought would be most relevant to share.

My motivation for writing this book was not to explain how to teach or lead. Instead, I hope to encourage conversations and reflections within our communities amongst those who share my passion for education. This is not a book that needs to be read straight through from beginning to end. Rather, I've arranged blog posts into chapters based on specific topics that I feel are important in education: school culture, relationships, curriculum and instruction, supporting teachers, working with families and the community, and the future of education. I added a short introduction to each chapter as well as a note to explain the context of each blog post. To encourage readers to think back on their own experiences and ideas, I pose some reflective questions at the end of each chapter.

The process of bringing this book to fruition was challenging, but the motivation that kept me moving forward was my belief that we can elevate education through discussions here in Hawai'i and in our country. We should be creating educational experiences, which our students need now and in their future. This means reflecting and discussing how we can work together to improve teaching and learning in our schools. If we agree that our children deserve an educational system that will prepare them to be the leaders of tomorrow, we all need to be part of the solution to ensure that our schools are a priority. Our world is changing rapidly, and schools should be preparing students for their future. This means that we cannot keep teaching the way we were taught when we were in school.

Thank you for reading *Educating with Aloha*. Hopefully, it will help you reflect on your own experiences and encourage you to share your opinions and participate in discussions about important priorities in education. It will take all of us to become involved if we want to make positive changes in our schools. I hope you will join me on this journey. ♥

Note to the Reader

In February 2003, I was hired as the principal of Hale Kula Elementary School, a public school on a military base in Hawai'i. In April 2016, our school name was changed to Daniel K. Inouye Elementary School after the late United States senator who did so much for our military families and for education in Hawai'i. It is the same school; only the name changed.

CHAPTER ONE

A Culture of Aloha

"True change requires a focus on creating school culture that supports academic, social, emotional, and character development of children."
—*Maurice Elias, PhD*

It is said that we don't get a second chance to make a first impression. The culture of a school has a direct impact on first impressions. Imagine being someone new—a student, a parent, a new staff member, a visitor—coming to school for the first time. Does the campus look clean and inviting? Are you welcomed with a smile and friendly faces? Are the students socializing and conversing with each other? A positive first impression can be an indicator of a school culture where people feel valued for what they can offer.

Creating a culture of aloha—love, compassion, empathy, and respect—was my most important goal as a teacher. Every year was an opportunity to take each individual student with their own strengths and challenges and help him/her to become an integral member of our classroom community. It started from day one when we got to know each other in a safe environment where risk-taking and innovative ideas were encouraged. By the end of the school year, we were an *'ohana*, a family, where we supported and celebrated each other.

It was more challenging when I was a new principal. The school culture included a strong and rich institutional history as well as established staff who were somewhat cautious about changes, which would be imminent under a new leader. As a first-time principal, it was important for me to listen, to learn, and to engage people in conversation. I was able to visit classrooms, observe what was going on, and talk with teachers afterwards. At our first professional development session, our staff gave input on what they saw as the strengths of our school as well as changes they felt we should consider. They were honest and excited that they were being asked for their thoughts and ideas. I realized early on that together we could build on a positive culture that already existed.

Schools are more than just a place for academics. Schools are a microcosm of society. It is where students learn to navigate important life skills like how to get along with others, including those from diverse backgrounds and those who have different ideas and opinions. It's where they discover how to understand their own feelings as well as the feelings of others. It's where they are encouraged to pursue interests and gain confidence to become contributing members of their community. It's where they learn to ask questions, to explore and discover new information, and to share their learning through meaningful projects that address voice and choice. It is a place where parents entrust us with their most precious resource, their children. It is a place where students and staff need to feel safe—physically, emotionally, academically, and socially.

A strong positive culture, a culture of aloha, was essential to our school and had an impact on teaching and learning. Our students, our teachers, our staff, and the community all contributed to a culture where safety and the well-being of others was a priority.

A Safe School
October 27, 2012

Our staff, especially our custodians, did a great job of keeping our campus safe. They were dedicated to ensuring that any potential health and safety issues were dealt with immediately. I was always proud when I walked around our beautiful and well-maintained campus. Safety was an essential component of our school culture because we wanted our parents to have confidence that their children would be safe while they were in our care.

Safety was at the forefront when we made decisions. We shared expectations at school such as how to walk in hallways or what rules we would enforce on the playground at recess. We were proactive and carefully reviewed and revised safety manuals as new information or new situations arose.

Sometimes, however, it takes an actual emergency situation to realize that even our best-laid plans needed to be revised. That was the situation back in 2012 when I wrote this blog post.

If we want to transform our school, we need to have a safe school. We need to assure parents that their children will be safe while they're in our care, and sometimes, it takes a "crisis" for us to reflect and to improve our procedures.

Schools practice emergency drills at least once per month. Most of the time, we have fire evacuation drills, but we are also required to have lockdown or shelter-in-place drills or school-wide evacuation drills. Our safety committee reviews our procedures and makes revisions to our plans after these drills. However, we never know what challenges we might encounter in a real-life situation.

This past week, we were placed on lockdown status by the US Army Garrison Hawaii as a precautionary measure due to a serious phone threat. Unlike a drill, which usually lasts no more than 30 minutes, this lockdown occurred for three hours, and it started during the second of three lunch periods. Additionally, one of our grade levels was on a field trip and would be returning to school shortly.

Fortunately, all of our staff pitched in to assist and provide support. Although we were never in danger, we are grateful that the US Army Garrison realized the importance of keeping our children safe. This lockdown provided us with an opportunity to get feedback from staff and to discuss concerns with our school community.

First and foremost, we need to improve our communication system—the military with the school and the school with the staff and school community. Thank goodness for social media! The US Army Garrison Hawaii continuously posted updates on their Facebook page, and I was able to inform parents through our school Facebook page. We also used the mass messaging system to let parents know that we were on lockdown status while reassuring them that we would keep their children safe. We communicated with staff via our phone intercom system but realized that we neglected to send email updates. That needs to be improved.

Second, we need to take care of basic needs: water, food, and yes, even toileting needs. A three-hour lockdown made us realize that we need to have a plan to ensure that our students have their basic needs met. Perhaps we can have water and nonperishable snacks for students to be kept in the classroom in case of an emergency, and yes, a discussion needs to take place regarding restroom needs because there are no toilets in the classrooms.

Third, our school opened in 1959, and because we live in Hawai'i, we have buildings that are spread out and open. This is great because we can take advantage of the trade winds to keep our buildings "natural" without the need for air-conditioning. However, the openness of our buildings also means that getting students from one place to another during a lockdown is a challenge, and with the windows and doors locked, the temperature in the rooms was sweltering. We need air circulation in the classrooms, and thankfully, installation of ceiling fans is part of our school-wide renovation plans, with completion in about three years.

I was so grateful to read all the parent comments on our Facebook page after the lockdown was lifted. Most of the comments were positive, and parents were grateful that their children were safe. Although they were anxious—after all, we are on a military base and many students have parents who are presently deployed—parents waited patiently across the street and calmly retrieved their children instead of panicking. A real-life situation like this is something I wouldn't wish on any school. However, I know that we will be better prepared if there is a next time, and hopefully, the lessons we learned can help other schools as well.

Schools are more than just a place for academics. Health and safety concerns will always be a priority and must be addressed promptly.

A New and Renewed Commitment
January 5, 2013

Much had changed between the time when I became the principal of Hale Kula in February 2003 and when I wrote this blog post in January 2013. I realize how my vision and the culture of our school were reflective of my core values, which were nurtured in me from the time I was a youngster growing up in Whitmore Village. Those values didn't change when I became a principal; if anything, they became more important as we confronted challenges that required us to make decisions based on what was best for our students. Three simple statements: Take care of yourself. Take care of others. Take care of our community. They are so global that they can be applied to almost any situation. Most importantly, our students could understand that their actions—positive or negative—could impact others. A positive school culture is contingent on people taking care of themselves, taking care of others, and taking care of their school community.

Blogging is not easy and takes more time than I anticipated. However, it's been a great way for me to reflect as a principal, and with the start of a new year, 2013, I am renewing my commitment to this blog and hope to reflect more regularly.

Next month, I will be at Hale Kula for ten years! So much has changed over this decade, but I believe that my core values have played an integral part in my commitment to the principalship and to the relationships I've fostered over the years. As we begin a new year, let me share three important statements that guide me in the work I do.

Take care of yourself. Everyone at Hale Kula gives 100% and more to their job. I certainly appreciate their dedication. However, the job will always be there, and there will always be something else that needs to be taken care of, so at the end of the day, it is important to remember to spend time with family and friends doing things we want to do with people who love and care about us. We also need to take care of our health by eating right, exercising, and finding time to relax and do the things that make us happy. This is something I learned while my children were growing up, and I have never regretted my decision to make our family my priority. Now that I am older and my kids are grown, I have more time to devote to my job, but I still make time to go golfing on the weekend, pamper myself with a pedicure, or go out to dinner with my husband.

Take care of each other. Education used to be a lonely job where the teacher was solely responsible for what went on in the classroom. Today, we know that collaboration and communication are important skills for our students and for our staff. Getting along with others is a crucial life skill, and working together, we problem solve and share successful ideas to improve teaching and learning. At our school, where 99% of our students are military dependents, this is even more important because for many of our families, the school is a critical system of support. This means providing academic, behavioral, and emotional support for those who need it—children and adults.

Take care of our community. The school is an integral part of the larger community, and our students are taught valuable lessons in caring for others and caring for our world. Unit studies, for example, share the importance of sustainability or the impact we have on our oceans and reefs or the reasons why we encourage reducing, reusing, and recycling. We have contributed thousands of canned goods or nonperishable food to the food bank; students donated to the Laulima Giving Project; we donated books to the Schofield Acute Care Clinic; students did chores around the house to earn money to donate to a Hurricane Sandy fund; and they pick up trash to beautify the campus or tutor younger students. These are just a few examples of how we care for the greater community, to make this world a better place for the future.

Although much has changed since I was a rookie principal, one thing hasn't changed. The people at Hale Kula—the staff, the students, the families, and the community—are the reason why I continue to love my job.

My Vision for Hale Kula
August 11, 2013

I wrote this blog post back in 2013 as part of my participation in the School Administrators Virtual Mentor Program (SAVMP). When I saw an opportunity to sign up for this program, I hesitated even though I knew I met the desired qualifications, which were that I blog regularly and that I was already a school leader. I realized that this program was an opportunity for me to step out of my comfort zone and to connect with both new and experienced administrators in other parts of the country and the world. I hoped to reflect and learn from other school leaders and to share blogs with my mentees as well as others within the SAVMP community.

It was an additional responsibility that required a commitment for one year, but I viewed it as an opportunity, and it definitely made me a more reflective school leader. I learned so much from our virtual community. Reading blogs from both experienced and newly appointed school leaders made me examine my own practices and gave me ideas about how I might approach challenges in the future. I appreciated the comments and questions from others in SAVMP. I realized the true value of a blog as an avenue to learn from others.

Recently, I took a risk and signed up to participate as a mentor in the School Administrators Virtual Mentor Program (SAVMP). Creator George Couros shared that he expected to get 35–50 requests to participate. He got 350! I was assigned to mentor three new administrators—from the United States and Canada—and I look forward to learning with my mentees as we go through this school year together.

This week, George suggested we blog about our vision for our school. As school leaders, we need to be the keepers of the vision, always bringing decision-making back to the core of our beliefs about our school and where we are headed.

When I was interviewed for the principal position at Hale Kula back in 2003, I was asked about my vision for the school. I remember sharing that because most of our students are military dependents, my vision was that they would embrace the unique culture of our state while getting an education that would prepare them to be successful wherever they went after leaving our school. This remains my vision for Hale Kula despite the changes in policies, changes in standards, and changes in personnel at the school, district, and state levels.

My vision is for every student to be successful while they are at our school and when they leave us to go elsewhere. I want them to be confident learners and to know that school is a safe place where they can share new ideas, learn new skills, and to sometimes struggle in the process, but to not give up. I want Hale Kula to be a place where:

- Everyone is included as part of a learning community, and every person is valued for their strengths.
- Everyone strives to be the best they can be and where we support each other to achieve our goals.
- There is a genuine attitude of caring for each other.
- Learning is meaningful and relevant to the real world, where students apply skills and strategies they have learned to complete relevant assignments.
- Students and teachers collaborate on projects and assignments and take responsibility for their own learning.
- Students and teachers care about our community and strive to make a difference now and in the future.

Some of these kinds of teaching and learning experiences are already happening at Hale Kula. For example, our fifth grade Hope Garden is an example of sustainability, and students lead tours for the community during Earth Day activities. Our sea urchin project is a great example of how our students are making a difference. I love that our teachers understand how important these kinds of experiences are for our students. While Hawai'i may never become their permanent state of residence, the experiences our students are gaining will help them now and in the future. Hopefully, they will continue to be caring stewards of their environment and care for each other.

New Year's Day 2014
January 1, 2014

As a youngster, I didn't think too much about traditions and their impact on me as a person. Traditions were something we did every year to celebrate a special day. Now as an adult, a mom, and grandma, I realize how important traditions can be, both culturally and historically, because they add richness to our multicultural society.

I remember that in late December 2013, I was having some difficulty in finding the right words for this particular blog post. It was serendipitous that it was also the start of a new year, a holiday that was important to our ancestors. As I was busy preparing the ozoni *(a special soup made with mochi or rice cakes) for our extended family, I realized how I would approach this particular blog post, and once I started writing, the words flowed. This is one of my favorite blog posts as it brings back fond memories of my childhood.*

Last night, we had our traditional ozoni or mochi soup, something our family looks forward to every New Year's Eve. Today, we'll be going to Mom's to celebrate with our extended family. New Year's Day was always a special holiday for us, and it has its roots in Shogatsu, which our ancestors celebrated in Japan before immigrating to Hawai'i.

When we were little, we always did extra housecleaning before January 1. To this day, I feel guilty if we don't clean the house—including the windows and screens—prior to New Year's Day. I remember playing with firecrackers with our older neighbors in Whitmore Village. It was a ritual to scare away the evil spirits, and we looked forward to the day when we graduated from sparklers to firecrackers. We used a mosquito punk to light the fuse and had to throw it before it exploded. On New Year's morning, we got up, took a bath to start off the year, then had Mom's delicious mochi soup. I remember going to our grandparents' house to celebrate New Year's Day. We always wore something new, usually a dress we received as a Christmas present the week before.

Time passed, and some of these family traditions changed as grandparents passed away, children got married and had kids of their own, or relatives moved. Fireworks require a permit now as we are more health-conscious and worry about the air quality and noise pollution, and we no longer buy them to scare away bad luck before the start of the New Year. As the younger generation start their own traditions with their own families, I wonder if our traditions, based on Japanese culture, will eventually fade away.

Like family traditions that began as part of our culture but changed over time, traditions at schools based on culture may be difficult to understand. We've been told that as a new leader, we should go in with our eyes and ears open so we can learn what the culture of the place is. We risk alienating those who may be offended if we come in as a new leader without understanding why things are done as they are. However, by moving forward respectfully with honest discussions, change is not just possible—it is necessary. Every school under new leadership has the potential to become better.

There have been many changes in the time I have been here as principal of Hale Kula Elementary School. In part, this is due to the increased expectations for schools to prepare students for a rapidly changing world. This is where knowledge of the culture of a place is most important. Is it a culture where the school community works together to address challenges? How do we communicate and work together to ensure the best teaching and learning environment for our students and teachers? Is there a climate where new ideas are embraced, shared, and discussed? What is the decision-making process at the school? Where do we leverage our resources so they have the greatest positive impact on our students?

Every school culture is a reflection of its community. At Hale Kula, our culture is a blend of our unique island culture and the transient nature of our military community. We believe that our school is an ʻohana, a family, and we treat each other with respect. This is especially important because most of our students are an ocean away from the support of their extended family. We believe in providing our students with an education that will prepare them to be successful now and in the future while also embedding an appreciation for the unique history and culture of our state. Finally, we want our students to understand the importance of taking care of our natural resources because their actions today affect our world tomorrow. Our students are global citizens, and their education at Hale Kula needs to prepare them for a rapidly changing world.

Just as influences beyond our control have impacted our family's New Year's traditions, the ways of doing things at a school may change due to changing times and/or changing leadership. A strong, positive school culture can determine whether the changes will be successfully implemented or not. As we move towards major changes in how we determine teacher and principal effectiveness and the impact on achievement, it is my hope that our school's strong culture of collaboration will translate to success for our students and teachers.

SOCIAL-EMOTIONAL SKILLS AS IMPORTANT AS ACADEMICS
September 7, 2015

When COVID-19 forced school closures for a lengthy period of time, a major concern was how to provide social-emotional support for students and the school community. An important part of being a school leader is taking care of others. At our military-impacted school, which is often a "pit stop" in a child's whole educational experience, we strived to ensure a safe and engaging school environment where students gained the skills and strategies to be successful, not just academically, but socially and emotionally as well.

At the time I wrote this post back in 2015, Peter DeWitt and I had been communicating for several years via email. I learned much from his blogs, his books, and his opinion pieces in Education Week. *Peter has written books about school climate and instructional leadership, and I agree with him that a positive classroom or school culture needs to be nurtured; it needs to be part of what we do daily. This was especially true at our school because we had new students registering almost daily, and they needed to feel that they were an important part of their classroom and school community. If we believe that everyone has something to contribute, we needed to welcome them into a safe environment where they could thrive. Accountability for our own learning starts with a feeling of belonging. This was something we focused on at our school and in our classrooms because it made a difference for our highly transient military-impacted students.*

Recently, Peter DeWitt shared a blog[1] about a recent experience. "You know what does suck?" he asks. "It's the way we talk about school." Peter does not hide the struggles he faced as a student, and I am sure his decision to become an educator is directly correlated to those school experiences. Many of his blog posts in *Finding Common Ground* speak of school climate, treating others with respect, and listening to what others have to say. I value his ideas and insights.

Recently, our school team discussed two articles/studies at our quarterly triage advisory meeting. This group includes our school team, district staff, and military partners from Tripler Army Medical Center and US Army Garrison Hawaii. The first was a longitudinal study that showed that military-connected students who had experienced multiple deployments of their soldier parents during the Iraq and Afghanistan wars were more at-risk for problematic behaviors. The second was a study that indicated that a child's social skills at age five were highly correlated with their success in adulthood. These studies were timely because this year, one of our strong focuses as a school is on continuing to improve our Positive Behavior Intervention Support (PBIS) system so that all students can be successful, socially and emotionally as well as academically.

We shared what we had in place to address the teaching of social skills and improving school climate.

- Our counselors work with students to share a Project Wisdom message over the intercom daily.
- We have school-wide agreements, and students can describe what each one means in the classroom or in the school.
- We have a conflict resolution process where students reflect on the causes and effects of their behaviors on themselves and others.
- Our school teams work together to review data and create behavior support plans for those students who may need more support to be successful in school.
- Our PBIS cadre meets regularly to review disciplinary data and to come up with school-wide activities to address areas of concern. We regularly update our PBIS booklet, and all teachers have a copy.
- We emphasize our Department of Education's General Learner Outcomes (GLOs), and we encourage students to set goals based on these GLOs. The six GLOs are:
    - Self-directed Learner (The ability to be responsible for one's own learning)
    - Community Contributor (The understanding that it is essential for human beings to work together)
    - Complex Thinker (The ability to demonstrate critical thinking and problem-solving)

- Quality Producer (The ability to recognize and produce quality performance and quality products)
- Effective Communicator (The ability to communicate effectively)
- Effective and Ethical User of Technology (The ability to use a variety of technologies effectively and ethically)

This appears to be a pretty good list of things we already do to address the teaching of social-emotional skills, but we can do much more. In this age, schools are rated based on high-stakes testing scores. As the aforementioned studies indicate, however, a school culture focusing on positive social and emotional skills is perhaps more important than just focusing on academics. So what can we do to improve what we already have in place at our school?

- Sharing the Project Wisdom morning message is not sufficient. We need to make sure students are discussing the message in their classroom and at home and perhaps set goals together.
- School-wide agreements and the General Learner Outcomes are important, but if students do not buy into them, they will just be another top-down mandate. If students co-construct criteria for what a respectful classroom or school looks like or what the GLOs mean, they will be more apt to hold themselves responsible for being part of a positive community of learners.
- We have been in classrooms where students co-construct criteria and hold themselves and each other accountable. It is wonderful to see and feel the positive climate in those classrooms, and students take responsibility for their actions. It is a safe environment, and when there is a problem, the whole class problem-solves together. In those classrooms, social and emotional skills are at the center, and academic learning revolves around it.

Here's what Peter DeWitt has to say in his blog post, "What Holds Us Back From Focusing on School Climate?"[2]

> There is no doubt that school climate is vitally important. When I work with educators in schools or school districts, school climate comes up as an important element to the social-emotional and academic growth of children. I feel that school climate is the plate which everything else, including academics, sits on. But too often it falls to the wayside and it becomes something where leaders act reactively rather than proactively.

As a military-impacted school, we have an obligation to ensure that our students are successful wherever they may move to in the future. Teaching academics via the standards is important, but perhaps we should be doing more to teach social and emotional skills, which can lead students to be more successful in the future.

POOR ROLE MODELS FOR OUR CHILDREN
March 12, 2016

Studies show that social-emotional learning is essential to developing positive behaviors in students. This is why schools make time during the day to teach students to advocate for themselves, to treat others respectfully, to work cooperatively with their peers, and to be kind to others, especially to those who may be experiencing challenges. When students ask tough questions, we need to have discussions, especially when they question the behaviors of others, including adults. Those discussions can teach students to listen to other viewpoints and to learn how to disagree respectfully without resorting to name-calling or ridiculing those with different opinions. It is important for us to honor our students' opinions and to let them know that they can speak up when they disagree.

It starts with the principal. If the principal treats the staff with respect, the staff will treat the students and their colleagues with respect, and students will be respectful to the staff and to their fellow students. It will trickle down to our parents and visitors as well. A positive culture of respect is essential to the well-being of the school.

Although I didn't want to turn my blog into a political commentary, I was very concerned about the way some candidates in the presidential race were putting others down with their toxic words. I felt very strongly that this set a bad example for our students, and that is why I opted to write this post back in March 2016.

As a lifelong educator, I believe that we have a responsibility to help our students become empathetic and contributing citizens in this ever-changing world. If we believe that every child can reach his/her potential to do something meaningful with their lives, then everything we do as adults should send that positive message to the child. Parents, relatives, neighbors, teachers, coaches, community leaders—we all help to mold our children into the adults they will become. That is an awesome responsibility and one I take seriously as a school leader.

We teach our students about mutual respect, no put-downs or name-calling, and taking care of ourselves and others. We want them to be able to solve their problems by talking with the other person and resolving their disagreements respectfully. We want them to show tolerance for differences of opinion or ideas.

As adults, we need to model the behaviors we want our students to internalize. To me, that is one of the most important responsibilities we have as educators and leaders in our classrooms or school or community.

And that is why it bothers me when I see what is happening in our election for president. This isn't leadership. It's bullying, name-calling, disrespect, and mob mentality. What do our children think when they see adults behaving as they do? How do we justify this kind of behavior from adults who claim they are qualified to be the leader of our country? We can't.

But if our children see that behavior and ask about it, we can use this as a learning opportunity. Turn the question back on the child. "What do you think?" Have them reflect on what they're seeing and hearing. Have an honest discussion with them—not a lecture—but a two-way discussion.

With the preponderance of coverage via news and social media, we can no longer shield our children from the kinds of disturbing scenes and speeches that are shared every day. But we can teach them about respect, tolerance, and kindness; and hopefully, the lessons they learn at school or at home or in the community when they are young can help them make the right decisions when they become adults.

A respected leader doesn't pull oneself up by putting others down. Let's hope that the adults perpetuating these behaviors will realize the negative impact they are having on the youth of our country.

What Is Happening?
March 16, 2019

Back when I wrote this post in March 2019, I was concerned that adult leaders were setting poor examples for our children when they disagreed on important issues and refused to compromise. Schools should be places where students learn to discuss important issues, listen to other viewpoints, look for compromises, and agree to disagree respectfully. They should be looking to adults to learn these skills.

Our staff did not always agree with my decisions as school principal, but the rational way to deal with that was to have open, collaborative discussions to try to resolve our differences of opinion. We may not have come to a win-win, but treating others' ideas with respect is essential to moving forward on our vision for the school. The negative impact on our school community would be difficult to overcome if ideas were ridiculed or dismissed without discussion.

We grew up learning the Golden Rule: treat others as you would want to be treated. Our world would be a better place if everyone remembered this.

One of my favorite quotes is a Native American proverb: "We don't inherit this world from our ancestors. We borrow it from our children." As a parent, a grandparent, an educator, and someone who believes in leaving this world a better place for our children, I am concerned about the state of our nation and our world.

What happened to common decency, to treating others respectfully even if we don't agree on an issue? We teach our children about respecting other people's opinions and how we sometimes need to listen to what they're saying and why they believe as they do. We tell them we can argue about an issue, but we still treat the other person respectfully. When there is disagreement, we can compromise and move ahead for the good of all. We don't condone name-calling, and we ask children to put themselves in the other person's shoes, to be empathetic to someone else because we don't know the challenges they are facing on the path they are walking.

At our school, we focused on teaching students tolerance, inclusiveness, and aloha. We realized the great impact we can have on our students' lives by showing them that open discussions can lead to deeper acceptance of others' ideas. We worked to include and accept all students and to listen to their viewpoints when there was disagreement. We would quickly address any concern before it became a problem, and we would never condone mob mentality where kids might get caught up in participating in actions they inherently knew were wrong. We used conflict resolution and delved deeper to find the root of the problem so the parties could move forward. We taught our students about the need to be careful that what we post on social media today is something we will not regret later.

As a nation, we can disagree on policies and politics, but we nevertheless should treat others with respect. We can argue our points vigorously, yet shake hands at the end of the day and seek to understand the other person's viewpoint. A difference of opinion doesn't mean that one side is right and the other is wrong; it means there can be a better outcome as a result of listening to another viewpoint and working together to find a better solution. Social media is a great tool for sharing ideas and to virtually connect with a wider audience, but our posts need to be respectful. And name-calling by adults is totally unacceptable; in fact, it is childish.

We have so many problems that impact our nation and our world including climate change, wars and conflict, poverty, racial divide, and economic challenges. We should be working together to make our world a better place, not causing a deeper divide between our people. We owe it to our children to leave them a better world than the one we inherited. Let's work together to make it happen.

A Culture of Aloha
Reflective Questions

- What are the health and safety guidelines that drive the decisions in your classroom or at your school? How might these guidelines impact your classroom or school culture?
- How does a positive school culture influence the actions when there is an actual emergency?
- What are your core values that guide you in your decision-making? How do these core values contribute to a positive classroom or school culture?
- What is the relationship between a school vision and school culture?
- How do your personal experiences impact the culture in your classroom or your school?
- How might a new school leader impact the culture of a school?
- How are social-emotional skills addressed in your classroom or at your school? What opportunities do students have to reflect on their progress on social-emotional skills?

- How can we, as adults, influence our students' perceptions about the culture at their school?
- Why is it important to have discussions when students question the behaviors of adults?
- Referencing Maurice Elias's quote at the introduction to this chapter, how does your school culture contribute to the academic, social, emotional, and character development of your students? ♥

NOTES

CHAPTER TWO

POSITIVE RELATIONSHIPS WITH OUR STUDENTS

"Never judge someone by the way he looks or a book by the way it's covered, for inside those tattered pages, there's a lot to be discovered."
—*Stephen Cosgrove*

Teaching is an art. Watching outstanding teachers is like observing a conductor, masterfully coordinating diverse musicians into an orchestra, playing increasingly more difficult pieces. It's taking a diverse group of students and turning them into a community of learners who each does his/her part to ensure the success of the whole. At the same time, it could be like watching a jazz performance where the teacher improvises, understanding that students' engagement during the lesson could take the activity to a whole different level or with a different focus. Just as jazz musicians improvise and create new sounds, these teachers recognize opportunities when interest in the topic more readily leads to engaged students and higher levels of thinking.

Whether the teacher is like an orchestra conductor or the leader of a jazz band, exemplary teachers understand the importance of nurturing positive relationships with their students. Their goal is to take each student where they are and to lead them on a journey that will take them farther than they thought possible as they navigate the school year. These teachers get to know their students—their strengths, their interests, their challenges—and use this information to build relationships. It starts with a smile and the promise of a fresh start each day, even if the previous day might have been rough.

As educators, we often think that students need to conform to our expectations, but every child is different. It is imperative that we get to know our students as people first if we want them to be contributing members of our classroom community. We focus on building relationships between the teacher and students as well as students with their classmates. Effective teachers understand what motivates students and who might need extra support in order to be successful. Their relationship with their students is what makes them effective as teachers.

In this chapter, I share stories about relationship building as well as concerns about what might be barriers to building positive relationships. This is especially true with students who may be experiencing challenges that are impacting their motivation to be in school. I also share about classroom management and working with students who may have challenges, which can impact positive relationships in a classroom. I end this chapter with a heartwarming blog post about a teacher and the positive impact she had on one of her students.

We sometimes have biases or misconceptions about how children learn, what they are interested in, and what their strengths and challenges are. In the end, the positive relationships as well as quality learning experiences and multiple opportunities for growth are what all students need.

ARE WE LOSING OUR BOYS?
July 9, 2012

This was the second blog post I wrote back in July 2012, and it was a bit personal for me because as the mother of three boys and the grandma of two grandsons, I worried about whether they would adapt to the expectations of their teachers when they started school. I had read books and articles about the differences between boys' and girls' brains and how boys often experienced challenges in the school setting. Thankfully, our sons and grandsons adjusted satisfactorily.

As a principal, I was concerned because our data validated that boys were more likely to be referred to the office for disciplinary reasons. They were also more likely to qualify for special education services. Because we had a strong support system in place, we did our best to provide services for those students—girls as well as boys—who were experiencing challenges in school. But I always worried that maybe we weren't doing enough.

As educators, we need to be careful about our biases or misconceptions about how children learn and what they are interested in. If we make erroneous assumptions, we rob our students of opportunities to explore and discover new interests. Quality learning experiences and opportunities are what all students need.

I worry that too many of our boys are not reaching their potential in our traditional educational system. Boys are disproportionately identified by teachers during the year as being behavioral challenges in class. I am concerned when I sit in on yet another meeting for a boy who meets the criteria for specific learning disability and is in need of special education services. Sure, there are challenging girls, too, but there are many more challenging boys, and our school statistics validate this statement.

I've read sobering statistics about boys' performance in school and the growing gap between the number of males and females who are graduating from college or attending graduate school. What can we do as educators to engage our students so that we can turn these statistics around?

Teachers have high expectations for themselves. They all hope that every one of their students will enjoy being in the class and learn what they need to be successful in the next grade level. Teachers spend countless hours planning for their class, and they sincerely hope their students will enjoy those lessons. It can be frustrating, therefore, when one or a few students upset the classroom with their antics or when they refuse to do their work. So much time is expended in attempts to get those students to comply; often, it is a battle of wills between the student and the teacher, and sadly, the student often wins. The result is that the student—usually a boy—starts to fall behind academically. Then, this student is labeled as challenging and difficult.

What can we do to change the statistics? The first step, I believe, is to build a positive classroom culture where all students feel valued as an integral part of our community of learners with something to contribute. Through the process of analyzing data and agreeing on and implementing team building and cooperative learning strategies in the classroom, we hope to see a decrease in behaviors that may be interfering with learning.

Building positive relationships means that teachers know their students as individuals—their interests, strengths, needs, learning styles, and what's happening in their personal lives. Knowing this information helps teachers as they plan engaging and relevant learning activities where students apply skills to create new learning for themselves. We can engage students by integrating different content area standards into an interdisciplinary or project-based unit, solving real-world problems, infusing research and technology skills to answer student-generated questions on a topic, and allowing students to create projects using a variety of tools to share what was learned. It won't be easy, but by providing an environment and professional development for teachers that supports 21st-century teaching and learning, we will hopefully see more engaged students in every classroom and fewer distractions to the learning process.

Our world is changing. If we don't change the way we teach and learn, we do a disservice to our students—boys and girls alike.

There Is a Fifth C
February 5, 2013

From the time our children are young, we give them choices. Do you want to wear the blue shirt or the red shirt? Which story do you want me to read to you? Do you want ice cream or a cookie for dessert? Giving children choices is a natural step in growing up and helps them to have some control over their own world.

What about our teachers? Oftentimes, we don't give teachers choices. We tell them what, when, and how to teach even though we know that all students are different and there is no one way to reach all students. When teachers see the value in having choice—choice in professional development based on their own needs, choice in how they structure their classrooms, choice in what resources to use—they will see the value in giving their students choices. The result will be more engaged and empowered students and teachers.

As educators, our classrooms are usually teacher-driven. Students are expected to follow the rules and the procedures that have been established by the teacher as a means of managing the classroom and the students efficiently and effectively. Classes are taught in blocks of time, and a schedule dictates what students will be learning at a particular time. Lessons are based on a common set of standards, students are given their assignments, and grades are allocated based on whether instructions were followed as well as the quality of the work. Many of us thrived in this system; we knew what we had to do to be successful in school.

Our 21st-century world is vastly different, and what worked back then may not be what our students need to be successful today. We read about how we need to teach the three Rs—reading, writing, and arithmetic—as well as the four Cs—collaboration, communication, critical thinking, and creativity—which describe the processes for teaching and learning as we move our teachers and our students forward in the 21st-century. Our blended learning pilot program, where fourth and fifth grade students spend part of the week in face-to-face learning and the other half accessing their curriculum and assignments online at home, is successfully demonstrating the power of the four Cs in engaging students in their studies.

But that is not enough. We found that even though we have a rigorous curriculum and students have multiple opportunities to use technology tools to demonstrate their learning through the four Cs, something else needs to be in place if we want our students to internalize and become self-directed learners, responsible for their own learning. The fifth C is choice. We have seen students in the blended learning class develop the attributes of a self-directed learner. They are able to view their assignments for the day or the week, prioritize how they will accomplish their tasks, and with guidance from the teachers, work on individual projects of their choice.

What is it about choice that can make the difference for students? Students in our blended learning classes have choices, although not all of them are "desirable" to every student. However, when students can choose how to prioritize and complete their assignments for the day, they learn organizational and time management skills. When they can choose a topic as part of their interdisciplinary unit study, they are motivated to research to find more information to answer their questions. When students have a choice on how to share their learning with others, their creativity and pride shines through their projects.

All teachers can and should provide choices for students—choices in *content* (What will I be learning? Why is this important? What are the big ideas and essential questions? What are the standards?), *process* (What resources will I use? How do I go about finding information? Will I learn better alone or in a group?), or *product* (How will I share what I learned? How can I get feedback from my peers? How do I know I have produced my best work?).

Recently, there has been much talk in the education world about giving students more choices in the classroom. Doing so can engage and empower them to become more self-directed, capable of learning on their own, not just in school. Choices can help students to be better managers of their time, to understand how they learn best, to help them to recognize what they are interested in or passionate about, and to make a difference for themselves and for others. We see it in stories that share about young people helping others by volunteering to do beach cleanups, assisting at food kitchens or homeless shelters, collecting pet food and supplies for animal shelters, or doing service projects that benefit others.

By providing opportunities to demonstrate the three Rs and the five Cs, students will gain skills and strategies to be confident, competent, self-directed learners. That's what we hope for for all of our students so they can be successful, not just in school, but in life.

CHRONIC ABSENTEEISM = A BIG PROBLEM
March 10, 2013

Our Department of Education made chronic absenteeism a data point for school success, so we set a goal as well as a plan to address student attendance in school. Yet, I was conflicted. My own gut feeling was that if we made school an engaging place to be, students would want to come. That is the question we need to ask ourselves. Do our students want to come to school? If the answer is no, we need to follow up with "Why?" and work together with the school team and the family to make school a desirable place for that student. If the answer is yes, we need to find out why the student is chronically absent, and home and school can team up to address that problem. There is no easy solution.

There are those who believe that chronic absenteeism is correlated to student achievement, but we found that was not always the case. We had students with poor attendance who did very well on assessments even if they missed important instruction as well as class assignments. Although we tried to get to the root of the problem, we were not always successful.

The recent COVID-19 pandemic forced schools to create asynchronous and synchronous learning environments using technology to share learning experiences and assignments. Some students who were chronically absent or not engaged during face-to-face learning thrived in a virtual environment. This is a great time for schools to discuss options that include blended learning or virtual learning for students who might be more successful and engaged in a different environment.

I recently returned from a family vacation to celebrate my dad's 88th birthday. It was wonderful, and I am so glad I took the time off from school to be with our family for this very special event. Of course, between email and texting, I was still tethered to my responsibilities as the principal at Hale Kula. After all, I didn't want to come back to work and have to catch up with the hundreds of emails I receive daily!

This vacation led me to reflect on something that has been a challenge at our school—attendance. We know that students need to be in school in order to maximize their learning opportunities. Last year, 16% of our students were chronically absent, defined as missing more than 15 days in the school year. In other words, 16% of our students missed about one whole month of learning. This is unacceptable, and we are implementing a variety of programs to reverse this trend including incentives for those who have perfect attendance for the quarter, informing parents more regularly, and asking for suggestions from our school community. However, our data suggests that these incentives and procedures are not having as positive an impact as we had hoped.

Because we are a military-impacted school, our families have different challenges that affect school attendance. With no extended family here on-island, a parent may not have the support when a child in the family gets sick (and there's no way to get the student to school) or the soldier is deployed or in training. When the soldier comes back from deployment or for R & R, families want to spend the time together or take a trip back home to spend time with their extended family. My vacation with my family reinforced that this is valuable time, and even if we would prefer students to be in school, we understand the importance of reunification, especially when a parent has been in harm's way.

So what can we do to ensure that students balance school and home needs effectively even if they are not physically in school? Since our families are transient, we need to make sure that the loss of instructional days does not result in learning gaps, which can impact students now and in the future when they enroll in a new school. Besides implementing incentive programs, we need to send a consistent message to parents about the importance of students coming to school regularly and keeping up with their lessons, and technology can be used effectively for this purpose.

We have encouraged all of our teachers to post their assignments as well as learning resources on their class websites. Additionally, we have licenses for programs such as Dreambox, KidBiz3000, and Measuring Up Live,* which are web-based, and other resources are available on our library web page, which students can access anywhere, anytime from any computer. We are moving towards cloud-based computing via Google apps; students will be able to work on their assignments and keep in touch with their teachers even if they are not physically in school. Our blended learning program is providing us with resources we can use with our fourth and fifth graders, and we should share similar resources for the other grade levels as well.

Our message to our parents is this: we understand the challenges of being a military family, but we need to work together to ensure that our students—your children—will be ready for the next grade level whether they remain at Hale Kula or move to another school in our state, our country, or the world. As a school, we need to have better procedures so parents understand that we are a team and that keeping up with schoolwork is essential even if a family is on a well-deserved vacation. This also means that parents need to set aside time during vacations so students can complete their assignments to ensure that they don't fall behind.

Our goal is to decrease chronic absenteeism at our school from

16% to 11%. It will take a collaborative effort to accomplish our goals, but we are determined to do all we can to reach our target so that all students continue to progress and have the skills and dispositions to be successful.

* When I wrote this blog post, we had licenses for these online resources. By the time I retired, we no longer purchased licenses. Student usage had declined and as a school, we agreed that there were other priorities that would have a greater impact on student learning.

MAKING CONNECTIONS AND BUILDING RELATIONSHIPS
August 12, 2013

Relationship building is a critical component of school culture. Teachers work to build community in their classrooms through team building or get-acquainted activities with the goal of getting students to know each other better and to find commonalities that make it easier when it is time to work together. Knowing another person's strengths and challenges as well as their likes and dislikes can be helpful when we are assigned to work in groups or teams to complete a project or assignment.

This blog post primarily focuses on working with our teachers; whenever we had the opportunity, we modeled relationship building. We wanted our staff to realize that they could do similar types of activities to build connections with their students. Starting the year on a positive note while building relationships is essential with our faculty as well as in classrooms with students.

The school year is off to a great start! This is going to be a challenging year due to a new teacher evaluation system, a new way of determining school proficiency, and new expectations for school administrators. It was important to get the school year off to a positive start!

A number of our teachers were busy this summer, attending conferences, trainings, and participating in professional development opportunities. Our blended learning team was fortunate to attend the International Society for Technology in Education conference in San Antonio; others attended AVID training; one of our teachers attended the Exxon Phil Mickelson Teacher Academy for Math and Science, and another attended a training at the Library of Congress on how to use primary resources in our teaching and learning. Additionally, teachers attended the Kamehameha Technology Conference, and others participated in training for Achieve 3000 or Thinking Maps. I mention this, not just to share the professionalism of our teachers in trying to improve their instructional practices, but to show how we needed to connect all of these trainings to ensure that teaching and learning at Hale Kula is meaningful and engaging.

With the statewide implementation of the Educator Effectiveness System, teachers will be evaluated based on five components. Our goal is for all of our teachers to be successful because we know that an effective teacher in the classroom has the most significant impact on student performance and student achievement. Therefore, we needed to make connections and to realize that by working together with our colleagues, we have a better opportunity to ensure that all of our students and teachers are successful.

Planning our first day agenda takes a lot of thought. I wanted to make sure we had time to make connections between the Educator Effectiveness System and other initiatives from the State, district, complex, or our school while building relationships at the same time. With a relatively large faculty (about 75 teachers) and a lack of designated school-wide professional development days for the past few years, new hires often did not have opportunities to meet or work with other grade level teachers. For this reason, it was important to use our administrative time wisely.

Earlier this summer at the Kamehameha Tech Conference, we had the pleasure of hearing and meeting Nirvan Mullick, who produced a video called *Caine's Arcade*.[3] I watched the video several times, and I knew that I wanted to share it with our teachers, too.

Caine's Arcade was the perfect video to discuss problem-solving and the attributes of a problem solver, and while we all agree that Caine is bright and creative, demonstrates perseverance and definitely is a critical thinker and problem solver, as educators, we often don't give our students these kinds of opportunities in the classroom. I considered having material available so teachers could work in teams to create something out of cardboard, but a Cardboard Challenge would take too long. What kind of activity would be shorter, a little less open-ended, but still engage our staff to work in teams while problem-solving?

Our librarian/media resource teacher shared the Marshmallow Challenge[4] with me, and I knew it would be just right for our purpose! Teachers worked in teams of four; the teams were put together ahead of time, and partway through, we removed at least one teacher from each group and had them switch with another teacher. We had puzzled looks, and teachers shared that they thought they had done something wrong when we asked them to switch groups. Some didn't want to change because they were comfortable with their group, and they were actually a little upset.

After reflecting on the experience, we had teachers complete a form to collect comments. One of the reflective questions we asked was, "How did it feel when you were asked to move to a new group, and how did you fit into your new group?" We wanted teachers to make the connection between how they felt as a newcomer in the group and how our students feel when they transition into our school since each year we have several hundred who transition after school begins. I loved this teacher's comment: "When I got switched to a different group, I thought about kids who come into our school as new students. It made me reflect on my experiences as a teacher welcoming new students."

After this uplifting, fun activity, our teachers were more engaged and participatory during our mandatory training. Continuing to build on the new relationships they were forming, teachers worked in groups, jigsawed the required assignments, and shared what they had read to ensure that everyone got the same information. They then posted comments, questions, or feedback on sticky notes on an app.

This reminds me of something a trainer said to us during our training this summer: Why do we leave the fun activities till the end of the day or the end of the week IF we have time? Perhaps if we mix it up and occasionally give students engaging assignments at the beginning of the day, we would have fewer tardy students since they wouldn't want to miss out on an enjoyable activity.

CLASSROOM MANAGEMENT AND BEHAVIOR CHARTS
July 8, 2014

This blog was written at the start of the 2014–2015 school year. The previous year, I had read several blogs about behavior charts, and I decided to share my thoughts with our kindergarten teachers. They were a diverse but cohesive grade level group that had agreed on certain routines and procedures such as using a traffic light system (green = a good day; yellow = mostly good; red = not a good day) to monitor classroom behavior. While 90% or more of the students could report to parents that they were on green at the end of the day, there were a few who consistently were on red. These students often lacked the social-emotional skills that are expected in school.

I did not tell the teachers to get rid of their behavior charts. Rather, I wanted them to discuss and reflect on whether these charts were necessary as part of their classroom management system. I also felt that any system needed to include recognition of positive behaviors. I realized that these kinds of behavior management systems could be trauma-producing for those students who needed more positive affirmations, not public shaming.

Classroom management can be the most challenging obstacle to learning. When the lesson is constantly interrupted so the teacher can discipline students, it takes away from the flow of the lesson, and valu-

able learning time is lost. This is why I advocate for strong relationships with students. When students are engaged and feel included in their classroom, there are fewer disciplinary disruptions.

Positive classroom management is so important to teaching and learning. Students are more responsive and able to learn together when there are structures, relationships, and procedures in place, but they don't have to be punitive.

Students will learn more when they are invested in and contributors in their classroom community. Classroom management is one of the components of our State's observation protocol for teacher evaluations. We have been in classrooms where the teacher planned a wonderful lesson that fell flat because students were not engaged or invested.

As a classroom teacher, I tried so many different strategies to ensure that my students would "behave." I gave out tickets to students to trade in on Fridays; it was too much work, and the students and I grew tired of it. I wrote names on the board of students who were misbehaving, and there was a series of "punishments" if they got so many checks. The same kids always had their names on the board, so I stopped that. I flipped it and started writing names of "good" kids, those who were ready before everyone else, who helped out another child, or who did something positive. That was better; at least I was rewarding students and not punishing them. Then I tried giving points to teams; this lasted longer because peer pressure was somewhat effective for most students. However, certain teams would rarely earn points because they were saddled with the kid who didn't care. This often led to a feeling of frustration at having "that kid" on our team. When I saw another teacher with a traffic light system, I tried that, too, with pretty good results. My recollection is that only one student was placed on red light that whole year. I think his mother was more devastated than he was.

After that, I went into administration, never discovering the "perfect" classroom and behavior management system. As I visited classrooms and spoke with teachers, it was evident that there were many different systems in place, and some worked better than others. But was it the system, or was it the teacher? Last year, I made the decision that any behavior management system needed to include opportunities for students to be rewarded for positive behaviors and not just moved down for "negative" behaviors. I was concerned that the first question I heard parents ask their kindergartener at the end of the school day was, "Were you on green today?" And it bothered me when parents requested a classroom change because "my child is on red every day." I really thought that if we started looking for opportunities to recognize positive behaviors in a child, the classroom climate would be so much more pleasant. Was it successful? For some teachers, it was, but for others, it didn't really matter if there were three colors or five. There were students who still got on red more often than not.

As a principal, I want to see well-managed classrooms where students are happy and meaningfully engaged and empowered through challenging activities. I have been in classrooms where the teacher never raises her voice, where students help each other, and a compliment by someone else—a visitor, another teacher, a parent, the principal—means a marble added to the class jar, which, when filled, means a special prize for the whole class. There is no individual chart where students are supposed to feel bad about being called out for inappropriate behaviors.

Often, an individualized behavior chart can have the opposite effect of what is expected, creating an "I don't care" attitude that can lead to a butting of heads between the teacher and that student. This student then is labeled as "challenging" and may be recommended for counseling services or is referred to the office to speak with an administrator.

Changing teachers' mindsets about behavior management can be difficult, but I realize that is part of my responsibilities as an administrator. We need a discussion about the best way to get students to want to be positive contributors to their classroom. It starts with including them as an integral part of their classroom community and knowing our students so we can fully engage them as learners. In other words, we need to build positive relationships with all of our students if we want them to gain the most benefit from the time they spend in our classroom.

A Network of Support
February 14, 2016

Back in 2001, when I was first hired as a vice principal, I often had a line of students waiting to see me for disrupting the classroom or not following classroom or school rules. I quickly realized that I needed to do something; I didn't want to spend my whole day disciplining the same students who were referred by the same teachers. I was fortunate to attend a professional development series on positive behavior interventions. I went back and inputted all the referral data into a website. When I shared that data with our faculty, we realized that we needed to change what we were doing. We asked tough questions as we looked at trends. Where and when were the most referrals occurring? Which students were being referred? Which teachers might need support with classroom management? Our staff discussed how we could address areas of concern through positive interventions, using data as our guide.

I remember that as a new teacher, I read that the word "discipline" means "to teach." As a principal, I shared this with our staff and with parents. We are not there to punish students; we are there to teach them expected behaviors and help them to be successful students.

This blog post was not easy to write but thinking about some of the students we were dealing with made me realize that it was an important topic to reflect on. Although it was written in 2016, what I wrote was the culmination of many years of learning and working together as a team to provide a network of support for those students who needed more guidance and tools to deal with challenging behaviors. In the end, working together as a home/school team made the biggest difference for those students who struggled the most.

As an educator for over 40 years, I've seen my share of students who had behavioral challenges in school. Some were as young as kindergarten, and others were older. They are the ones who needed to be removed from the classroom because their behavior disrupted teaching and learning or who bolted from or left the classroom without permission, eliciting a sometimes frantic "Code Nike."

Most students do comply with the rules of school. A reprimand and communication between the teacher and parent usually has its intended consequence, and students realize that we have rules because we want a safe and nurturing learning environment.

It's that small 1–2% of students who pose the most challenges, who make up the bulk of our disciplinary referrals, and who often require a team effort to get that child to a frame of mind where he/she is ready to get back to learning.

As part of our Positive Behavior Intervention System, we do our best to ensure a classroom culture where students work and succeed together. Making sure that all students are engaged and learning takes special skills, and it can be especially difficult for a teacher when one student takes up so much individualized attention because of his/her disruptive behavior.

I certainly don't have all the answers, but my experiences as a parent, grandparent, teacher, youth sports coach, and administrator have taught me a few things about working with our children who have the most challenging behaviors.

- I believe that all children want to be loved. Unfortunately, some children come from backgrounds without the kind of love most of us knew growing up, or they have been hurt or abandoned before and don't want to be hurt again. The result is that these children don't know how to accept love or to give love in return. Our job as educators is to not give up on these challenging children. If we can break through their tough exterior, we may help them realize that there are people who care and who want them to

succeed.
- Children need boundaries and rules. Rules help us to feel safe. School is a great place for students to learn that there are rules to be followed, and that there are consequences when we don't follow those rules. Consequences don't have to be punitive; natural consequences work as well as or better than negative consequences in many situations.
- Children know when someone likes them or not. As adults, we need to separate the child from his/her actions. We may not like what they did, but we can still like them as a person.
- We recommend giving six positive comments to every negative comment. Sometimes, that can be difficult to implement, but students who have difficulty with their behavior in school are the ones who need the most positive affirmations. We should make a special effort to catch those students when they are doing what is expected and show them our appreciation.
- Examining and analyzing the data as a team can help us to figure out what might be triggering the negative behaviors. We can then create a plan to teach appropriate strategies to eventually extinguish those negative behaviors. Being proactive rather than reactive can make a difference, not only for the student but for the sometimes frustrated and exhausted staff as well.
- Our counselors, behavioral therapists, resource teachers, grade level colleagues, and administrators should all be a part of a child's safety net, especially for those students who are experiencing behavioral challenges in school. We should know which children to check up on from the time they enter in the morning until the time the day is over. "Hey, how are you doing? How's it going?" from multiple staff members sends a message to the child that people care.

- As a school with a highly transient student population, we don't necessarily know our students' histories before they enroll at our school. Cumulative records don't always tell the whole story about a student. Often, a child with major behavioral challenges is also struggling academically. The question then is, "Which do we address first? Behavior or academics?" Our support team has come to the conclusion that we need to address both behavior and academics through targeted and focused interventions. Addressing behavioral challenges may mean that the student is more willing to put forth effort on academic tasks, and when the student is more successful academically, we may see fewer behavioral incidents.

In my 40-plus years as an educator, we have had a few students who needed more intensive services than what we could provide at the school level. However, we have had many more stories of those who may have had challenging behaviors but through a network of support were able to become more successful. Those are the students who taught me the most, I think, about working as a team, having perseverance, building positive relationships, and never giving up on a kid.

THE DIFFERENCE A TEACHER MAKES
May 5, 2019

In promoting my first book, Leading with Aloha: From the Pineapple Fields to the Principal's Office, *I had the opportunity to conduct sessions with groups of teachers. Near the end of my presentation, I would read the Facebook post below by Carol Conway, and there were many tears. I ended by asking teachers how they wanted to be remembered by their students tomorrow, next year, or many years from now.*

As you'll see, relationships were important to Kathleen Lloyd. She knew her students and what they needed at the time they were in her class. She planned activities that would allow her students to put personal touches on what they were learning. I would hope that every educator has this kind of positive impact on his/her students.

A few months after I wrote this blog post, and after celebrating her 100th birthday on May 3, 2019, with her family, friends, and some former students, Kathleen Lloyd passed away peacefully at home. She is remembered with fondness.

Last Friday (May 3, 2019) was the 100th birthday of a special lady whom I had the privilege to meet last year at our family reunion in San Jose. Kathleen Lloyd is the mother of a cousin's husband, and she and other family members who live in the area joined our Amemiya clan to share stories and make new memories. When I was introduced to Kathleen, she shared that she had been Facebook friends with our son Jarand, who had recently passed away. I immediately invited Kathleen to be my friend on Facebook. She accepted.

I was scrolling through my FB feed on Friday and saw this post from Carol Conway. It resonated with me; I wasn't aware that Kathleen had been a teacher in her younger days. I read that post several times and knew that I wanted to share it. I messaged Carol, and she agreed to let me use her post in my blog. Thanks, Carol!

> Do you remember fifth grade? For me, it was 1973–74, my father had died the year before and my mom, I'm sure, was struggling to keep us in our Mill Valley home. (She succeeded—thanks Mom!)
>
> My fifth grade teacher celebrated her 100th birthday today, (and she's on Facebook!) so I tried to pry a few memories from the dark recesses of my creaky brain.
>
> I remember the garden that Mrs. Lloyd started on our school grounds. She taught us about growing

food in unyielding soil. I remember learning how to do batik and making a lovely Douglas Iris on a purple background, which I turned in to a pillow. I remember going to Cronkhite Beach to gather pebbles to make mosaics, and finding a single carnelian that I used to make the eye of the snail I created.

In fifth grade I remember competing for the highest level in SRA—and winning. Mrs. Lloyd, I can picture the classroom, the tall windows facing south, and you sitting in front with an open book, looking out at us between paragraphs. I loved being read to—I have no surviving memories of what you were reading, but it was a quiet time for me when my world was tumbly, and I enjoyed it.

Mrs. Lloyd, I hope that you had a birthday full of the things and the people that you love. I hope that you know that your students felt loved and protected in your class, and that you made a difference. And I know that I speak for my brothers as well—David before me, Jeff after—you mattered to us.

Happy Birthday!

As I read and reread this tribute to a beautiful teacher, I had a few aha! moments. First, 1973–74 was my first year of teaching. I was just getting started in my career while Mrs. Lloyd was making lasting memories with her students. The second thing I noticed was that Carol remembers things like gardening and art and field trips. There's nothing in there about test scores or academics. (Hmm… what will students remember about their teachers 45 years from now?) Carol mentions SRA levels, something I remember from my seventh grade reading class where, like her, I quietly competed to get to the highest level before anyone else. (Someone beat me; I was second, but once I was done, I got to read whatever I wanted to in that class.) Lastly, Carol's recollection of being read to was so touching. Mrs. Lloyd was reading aloud to her students in the fifth grade, and Carol cherished and needed that quiet time when her world was "tumbly." (In today's classrooms, read-aloud time is often eliminated as teachers rush to "cover" the curriculum, but students may need that time to settle their "tumbly" world.)

This lovely post spoke volumes about the positive impact of a teacher on a student, one who was going through emotional challenges. Forty-five years later, this student shared these fond memories, and I am sure Mrs. Lloyd was touched. Henry Adams said it best: "A teacher affects eternity. He can never tell where his influence ends."

POSITIVE RELATIONSHIPS WITH OUR STUDENTS
Reflective Questions

- How do you nurture positive relationships with your students?
- Why is it important to create a trusting relationship with your students?
- What kinds of choices do students have in your classroom or at your school?
- How might giving choices help students to be more engaged in their own learning?
- How are behavioral expectations determined in your classroom?
- What are your options when students are not engaged in the lesson or activity?
- Think about a challenging student you had in your class. What worked with this student? Why did it work? What didn't work and why? What might you do differently if you had to do it over?

- How would you want your students to remember you 10 years from now? Twenty, 30, or 40 years from now?
- Think about Stephen Cosgrove's quote at the introduction to this chapter. Recall a student who was like a book with tattered pages. How did your relationship with that student change your first impression about him/her? ♥

NOTES

CHAPTER THREE

Explore, Discover, Create, and Share

"Much education today is monumentally ineffective.
All too often we are giving young people cut flowers when
we should be teaching them to grow their own plants."
—*John W. Gardner*

Have you walked into a classroom with excited, engaged, and eager learners? I have. I observed students discussing how to solve a problem or planning how to share what they were learning with the rest of the class. Maybe they were involved in a discussion about a book they were reading or researching information using technology about a topic they were passionate about. Students were respectful, able to listen to other viewpoints, and to have meaningful discussions. They worked collaboratively, ensuring that each person contributed to the learning. In these classrooms, the teacher was orchestrating the action, making sure students were on task and working collaboratively, offering thoughtful questions or comments to take learning to a higher or deeper level.

With school closures due to COVID-19, teachers suddenly were thrust into changing the way they taught from face-to-face, in-person teaching to virtual or distance learning via the computer. In the process, schools had to redefine themselves, and teachers had to figure out new ways to engage their students and ensure that they continued to learn. As educators, our job is to ignite a passion for learning. Students need to be proficient in skills such as reading, writing, and problem-solving because these skills are essential when exploring a topic they are interested in learning more about. It could be a question or an interest in mathematics, history, art, science, music, literature, languages, sports, or a myriad of other topics. Today, with technology so readily available and with mentors who are eager to support our young people, education can be much more meaningful for our youngsters.

Our school's vision was "Empowering learners to explore, discover, create, and share," a description of what we believe should be happening in our classrooms. In this chapter, I share about teaching and learning at our school. It started with our teachers, who were encouraged to be innovative and to try different strategies to engage their students, to collaborate with their colleagues, and to share what worked or what needed to be improved. We trusted our teachers to do their best for their students.

I loved writing about and sharing about teaching and learning via my blog! Although my experiences and these blog posts are geared for elementary schools, I believe they can be adapted for older students as well. Let's stop focusing on test scores and memorization as a measure of success. Instead, let's focus on deeper learning that sticks, learning that is meaningful for students.

SCIENCE IS AN ADVENTURE!
August 17, 2012

Every preschool and elementary school classroom should have a science center where students can explore and discover through observations as well as experimenting with different tools and materials. Children are naturally curious about their environment, and I loved seeing students outdoors at recess, watching spiders spin their webs or looking for sow-

bugs with their magnifying glasses in hand. They often pored over the pictures in an informational book about something they were interested in and would ask me to read the captions.

Too often we curb children's interest in learning more about things in this world because we don't give them a venue to explore the questions they are curious about. We need to let them explore things and discover how to find the answers to their questions.

This blog was written back in 2012, when we partnered with Dr. Richard Jones from the University of Hawai'i–West O'ahu. He received a grant to grow sea urchins that would be released to eat invasive algae that were destroying the coral reefs in Kāne'ohe Bay. Although it was a valuable learning experience for our students and teachers, it was also labor-intensive to ensure an environment where the sea urchins could thrive. After two years, our teachers reluctantly decided that we could not continue with the project, but we were able to release about 100 sea urchins in the ocean near the Waikiki Aquarium where algae were overtaking the reefs. Hopefully, we made a difference.

One week has passed since we got our sea urchins. It was somewhat traumatic—for the teachers. They are concerned that some of their urchins are dying, and they want to know if they're doing something wrong. The urchins aren't eating the specially designed food, and now that food is lying on the bottom of the aquarium. We don't have the right kind of scale, and we don't know if we're overfeeding or underfeeding the urchins. Dr. Jones is patient and reassures the teachers that this is normal. We didn't know how the urchins would do when they were moved from one environment to another, and we need to try the different foods to see if the urchins will eat them because later in the year, it'll be harder to get *limu* (seaweed). He encourages the teachers and tells them that they (and the students) are doing fine, and he concludes his advice with "Science is an adventure!"

Sometimes, as educators, we want everything to come out perfect. This is a new experience for us; we have never been part of a project using live animals, and we don't want our urchins to die. But as Dr. Jones shares, science is an adventure. That is why I appreciate that these teachers volunteered and are so immersed in this project. I smile when I read the questions and observations within our social media group, and I share the concern when things are still so unpredictable.

I learned science through textbooks. Suffice it to say that I don't recall much from my classes. When I was studying to become an early childhood educator, I was introduced to a new way of teaching science through hands-on experiences. Dr. Pickens from the University of Hawaiʻi provided an aha moment for me that I never forgot. "Science is a verb," he shared, and that changed my views as an educator about science.

I made it my mission to make sure that students were sciencing in my classroom. We encouraged exploration and discovery. We had tools like magnifying glasses, assorted magnets, balances, and even a stereoscope on the science table. Students brought in live bugs to feed the green anole lizard in the terrarium, and through their observations they discovered that even if sowbugs were plentiful and easy to catch, the anole lizard wouldn't eat them, so they had to find other food. We raised butterflies from caterpillars and toads from tadpoles. I won't forget a parent/teacher conference I had with a father who shared that on the first day of school, his first grader solemnly and very seriously stated, "I like Mrs. Iwase; she has a lizard skeleton on the science table."

Our Hawaiʻi schools are transitioning to the Next Generation Science Standards, and if implemented correctly, students will be actively sciencing rather than just learning science concepts through books. It will not be easy because many of us who became elementary educators do not have strong backgrounds in science.

Science is not just a subject or a content area we need to teach in school. Kids are naturally curious; let's encourage their interest in learning more about things in this world by giving them a venue to explore the questions they are curious about. We need to let them explore and discover how to find the answers to their questions. Stand and deliver is not enough; learning must be student-centered, relevant, and process-based. After all, science is all around us!

VIRTUAL LEARNING
December 10, 2012

We were fortunate to receive a Department of Defense Education Activity grant in 2011 to implement a blended learning program at our school. This was a proposal to address the overcrowded conditions in our classrooms when enrollment increased to over 1,000 students. Blended learning would allow two classes to share a room since students would come to school three days and access their curriculum virtually at home on the other days. We were actually ahead of our time in implementing this kind of program at the elementary level, and it was a successful experience for the teachers as well as the students.

Although the blended learning program was not sustainable once our grant funds lapsed, the lessons we learned helped us to encourage the use of technology in all of our classrooms. In fact, our goal was for all of our classrooms to be a blend of face-to-face and online or virtual learning where students would have ready access to technology or other resources to gain skills or information and to have the opportunity to share what they learned.

When we hear "1:1 initiative," it often means that every student has a device with preloaded instructional content and assignments. At our school, it meant that students had access to and could make decisions about their own learning using all the resources available to them. It meant that teachers were encouraged to try new apps or new programs to empower their students, because one size doesn't fit all. Teachers and students are individuals, and what may work for one may or may not work for others. It is the process of learning, of adapting, and of sharing that really encouraged our students and our teachers in their quest to be independent, self-confident learners.

In 2020, when the COVID-19 pandemic closed schools, virtual learning became a reality. Some teachers and students made the transition seamlessly because they already had systems in place. For others, it was a steep learning curve. I believe that when our teachers look back, though, they will realize how much they learned despite all the challenges they faced. Our students and our educational system will ultimately be the beneficiaries now that teachers have new strategies and tools that they can use.

Much has been written about 21st-century teaching and learning, but are schools actually using these strategies in their classrooms? We were fortunate to receive grant funding to pilot a blended learning program, which combines face-to-face learning with online learning. The fourth and fifth grade students in this program came to school three times a week and accessed their lessons online at home on the other days. We are still learning and revising, but here are a few lessons learned from this first semester.

- Although we had hoped to register 20 students from each grade level for the blended learning class, we had a little more than half that number. Parents were interested in learning more about the program, but they weren't willing to have their children be guinea pigs in this pilot year. This was a blessing in disguise; it gave us time to work out the kinks and to make changes if necessary. Additionally, according to studies, online teachers burn out more quickly than those who teach in face-to-face environments, and this is something we want to avoid. Our blended learning teachers are not available 24/7, but they do feel a responsibility to regularly communicate with their students and parents, and they are constantly checking for understanding with their students. Our teachers have stated that this year, they are truly partners in the teaching/learning process with the students and their parents.
- We decided that we wanted a rigorous curriculum that

addressed the Common Core State Standards as well as projects based on the grade level interdisciplinary units. Designing lessons to be placed online is challenging. Instructions need to be clear and not too lengthy.
Our teachers spent many, many hours with the course designer to ensure that the lessons and assignments were understandable for students. As they teach, teachers are constantly reviewing and revising their lessons. Although this is time-consuming, we believe that the curriculum our teachers created addresses the four C's of 21st-century learning—collaborating, communicating, critical thinking, and creating.

- In order to be successful in online classes, students need to be self-directed. This is one of our Hawai'i Department of Education's General Learner Outcomes, but until now, I don't think we truly defined what this means. As teachers, we often have control over our classrooms. Students are told when to listen and when to talk, when to work, when to turn in their assignments, where to turn it in, what to do for homework, etc. There is very little opportunity for students to learn to organize or manage their time, or even to have choices in their assignments or how to share their learning. The successful blended learning students learned to budget their time to get all assignments completed in the time allocated. They learned to prioritize, to be organized so they can track what they have completed and what they need to do next. They learned to ask for help, not just from the teacher, but from their classmates or from tutorials that are placed online for their use. They are able to choose their projects and to determine the best way to share what they learned. They are truly self-directed.

- If we want teachers to begin integrating technology seamlessly into their instruction, we need to provide professional development and mentoring and ensure that they have access to technology. One of the expectations of the blended learning teachers is that they will share and encourage their colleagues to use some of the resources that are available online for teaching and learning.

- Students are excited when they are able to use technology to learn something new and to use different apps or tools to share what they've learned. Therefore, they must have access as well as opportunities to share with their peers and to learn from each other.
- We need to prepare our students from the time they enter kindergarten. Technology is an integral part of their lives—both in and out of school—and waiting until they're "ready" is not going to help them down the road. Technology is changing so quickly, and an important disposition for students is adaptability/flexibility. We have seen preschoolers playing with their parents' mobile devices; we need to make sure all of our students have opportunities at school to use technology tools as important learning resources.

This first semester was a huge learning curve for our blended learning team, but work evidence and conversations with these students and their teachers have validated what I believe about teaching and learning—that students are capable of learning so much more when we give them the tools they need to succeed and provide an environment that values independence, interdependence, and individuality.

It's More Than a Place to Borrow Books
February 10, 2013

After I wrote this blog in 2013, a couple of exciting things happened. First, our librarian, Michelle Colte, was selected in 2014 as the first recipient of the K–12 School Librarian of the Year, an honor spon-

sored by School Library Journal. *What a well-deserved honor for Mrs. Colte to be chosen from all of the school librarians in our country! Mrs. Colte does more than just work with students and teachers. She plans school-wide activities and invites our families and the community to get involved. Book fairs are fun, family events; she coordinates activities like the Cardboard Challenge, Hour of Code, Global Read Aloud, Nēnē Award, lunchtime pop-ups where students teach other students, and most recently, video game design.*

Second, our new library media resource center was completed in 2016, and what a building it turned out to be! Much discussion and thought went into planning and designing this building; the goal was to create a space that can grow and change to meet the literacy and information needs of our students, teachers, and school community now as well as in the future. There are lots and lots of books to read, to borrow, and to love. There are construction toys and a paper roller-coaster that continues to grow as students come up with a new idea. A side room became an "Exploratopia," a favorite place for students to congregate, collaborate, and create during recess, lunchtime, and after school. There, they explore and discover new ways of using the myriad of materials in creative ways.

Yesterday, I was able to attend the annual conference for the Hawai'i Association of School Librarians, an organization committed to improving teaching and learning in our schools. This volunteer organization shares resources, provides professional development opportunities for educators, and is involved in the community as well by hosting events for students such as the Nēnē Award.

Our library is a vibrant place, filled with eager students who love to choose a "just right" book to borrow, but our library is more than just a place to listen to stories and learn how to find a book. Our library is a media resource center where students learn to access information about topics of interest, to use different technology tools to collaborate with their classmates, to communicate and share information with students at other schools, and to nurture a love of books and literacy.

Our school librarians need to change the way they provide services to teachers and students if they want to survive. This can be a challenging process. When we hired our librarian, she and I had lengthy discussions about our vision for the library. We wanted teachers to be present for the lesson so they could follow up in their classroom. The librarian needed to be a collaborator with the grade level teachers as they planned instruction based on big ideas and essential questions. We needed a vast collection of books—both fiction and nonfiction—and we wanted the books to be borrowed, not sitting on the shelf. As technology tools became more available, the librarian modeled the use of these tools in instruction so students and teachers could access and share information virtually as well as through traditional projects.

There are those who claim that students can get whatever information they want electronically, so libraries and print material are no longer necessary. I disagree. Just because information is readily available electronically does not mean that students know how to choose the right resource, how to skim and scan to find answers to their questions, how to take notes and organize them in a meaningful way, and how to summarize and share that information with others. That is why the librarian is an important resource at our school. Additionally, every child needs to experience sharing a book with a special adult. I remember those moments with my own sons, reading some of our favorite books together, laughing, crying, or just sharing that special time together. I believe that being exposed to all kinds of books—fiction and nonfiction—nurtures a love for reading that translates to greater success in school and in life. That's another reason why we need school libraries.

A school library or media resource center is just a building. No longer is it just a place to borrow books. What makes the library an interesting and vibrant place for learning is how the materials are used and the kinds of learning opportunities the library staff provides for the school community.

It would be a shame if school libraries suffered the same fate as businesses like Borders or Blockbuster, which did not realize the need to change to meet the challenges of a changing world until it was too late. Let's work to make sure that does not happen with school libraries and librarians.

Math Literacy
January 9, 2014

I enjoyed math when I was in school, but today I really don't remember much about the math classes I took in high school or college. The knock on math education is that it doesn't have much applicability in the real world. When I think back to my math classes, I learned formulas for how to solve a problem, but I never questioned why these formulas worked. Drill and kill. I was pretty good at it.

But math is much more than just getting the right answer to a problem. It's about knowing what the problem means and why an answer does or does not make sense. It means being aware of how we use math in our daily lives and why it is important. It is about discussing different strategies to solve the problem. It is about seeing the relevance of math in our lives. At the time I wrote this blog post in 2014, our school's focus for professional development was on math problem-solving. It was relevant and necessary but also quite frustrating for some of our teachers because it was so different from what we had been teaching.

One of my favorite activities at Hale Kula was when we asked our parents to tell us how they used math in their daily life. We had so many responses and we posted them all on a bulletin board in the front of the school. It was wonderful to see students reading and discussing different responses. They saw visually all the ways our parents use math every day at home, at work, or at play.

Just as science is all around us, math is, too. Students are much more engaged when they see the relevance of math in their daily lives.

We understand the relationship between fluency in reading and comprehension. We know that if a student has difficulty with decoding and struggles with sight words, reading fluency is negatively affected. The meaning of the sentence or paragraph is often lost when so much effort is spent on figuring out the words.

Likewise, students who have poor fluency in math facts will most likely struggle with problem-solving or other math application skills. The Common Core Standards for Mathematical Practice require students to be able to communicate their understanding and to use effective strategies to solve problems. Math is not just rows of problems with no relevance to real life. Math should be understood and discussed, much like we discuss literature.

Math problem-solving is one of the Mathematical Standards of Practice in the Common Core. We want our students and teachers to find beauty in solving challenging problems and seeing math all around us.

I reflected on why we are struggling with the problem-solving process. When we teach reading, we introduce skills and students apply those skills as they read—reading to learn something new, reading for pleasure, reading to answer questions, reading to understand. When students can apply their acquired reading skills to select books of their own, when they know how to find information about a topic they're interested in, when they can discuss a book or a story with others, or when they can persevere to make sense of a difficult passage or article, we are confident that they have the skills to be literate learners.

Yet we do not provide opportunities for students to apply math skills to real-world problems, which are all around them. We teach skills in isolation, and after students have practiced that skill and seem to understand the process, we move on to the next mathematical concept. We assign word problems that may or may not be realistic or meaningful to students. We play math games or read books about math or sing songs, but we don't give students the opportunity to apply the math skills in a meaningful way so students can make sense of why this is important to know and be able to do.

Rather than make up problems involving percentages or decimal points, why not have students look at newspaper ads to determine which store has the best value on a laptop or a Wii? Can we have students plan a meal and then determine what they will need to purchase at the market and how much that might cost? How about walking around the school and taking photos of different patterns they find and putting together a slideshow? Or bring in menus from a restaurant and have students figure out what they could buy with a certain amount of money.

Our fifth grade has an organic Hope Garden that is hands-on and project-based. Students learn science and social studies concepts; they research so they can post a comment to a question on their Hope Garden blog; they decide what they want to plant and why; and they do math. Lots of math. Students measure the plots and determine the perimeter and area of each plot as well as the whole garden. They do experiments and measure the growth of different plants. They predict how many ears of corn they will harvest and share their strategy. They weigh their harvest, decide on how to package what they've grown, and keep track of their expenditures and profits. All these different activities help students realize that literacy—reading, writing, and math—can be part of their everyday lives. This relevance is what makes the Hope Garden so popular with our fifth graders.

It isn't necessary to have an extensive project to teach math using the world around us. College and professional sports provide wonderful opportunities to present challenging problems. The score of the football game was 35–24. What different ways could the teams have scored their points? The Sochi Winter Olympics is coming up. Which country do you think will win the most medals? Why? Then keep track daily to see if any of the students will be right. There's a construction project going on at our school. How do the workers use math skills in their work? These are just a few examples of how we can engage students so they love math and see the relevance of math in their daily lives. We need students to persevere to solve challenging problems and to recognize that math is an important part of their daily lives.

Is Spelling Important?
August 14, 2014

I contemplated whether I should include this particular blog post in this book, but I realized that for many elementary teachers, spelling tests are part of their weekly routine. I remember sharing this blog with our teachers after I wrote it back in 2014. I asked them to think about whether those weekly spelling tests were helping students to be better spellers and writers. I know some teachers continued to do what they had always done, but others decided to change what they were doing to make spelling more meaningful or applicable for their students.

I hope that this blog post will make teachers reflect on why they continue to do things just because they've always done it that way. If we believe that higher level thinking and application of skills is more important, then let's examine what we expect of our students. What is the purpose of spelling tests if students cannot apply what they practiced to their daily writings? What is the purpose of spelling tests if a student already knows how to spell the word correctly? How can we give students the tools to check their own spelling in their assignments? These are some questions I'd ask teachers to think about.

I loved spelling tests when I was in elementary school. I was good at spelling and didn't even have to study to get good grades. So when I began teaching elementary school, I followed the lead of those who had been teaching that grade level for many years as well as what I remembered from my days in elementary school. We followed the spelling list in the Teacher's Manual for reading. The kids wrote the words down on Monday, wrote it several times in their spelling book for homework that night, wrote a sentence with each word the next night, alphabetized the list on Wednesday, and studied for the test on Thursday night. After the test on Friday, parents waited anxiously for the tests to be returned, and we had happy kids or sad kids, depending on how they did. Sometimes, parents would say, "We studied all night long, and he knew how to spell the word last night. I don't understand why he missed it."

I began to question the value of spelling tests. I was concerned that students were scoring 100% on Friday, yet they were misspelling those same words when they wrote in their journal or responded to a question the following week. I realized that I needed to rethink whether spelling tests were that important.

So I changed what I was doing. On Monday, the students would take a pretest, and if a student scored 90–100%, he/she was exempt from taking the test on Friday. They still did the homework, but these students didn't have to write the word several times in their spelling book. At least I was differentiating, I thought, but really, those spelling tests still bothered me. I also noticed that some students felt defeated; they were working so hard but still not getting the kind of scores they wanted. "Is spelling so important?" I asked myself. It would have been so easy to abandon spelling altogether and take the heat when parents questioned why. In the back of my mind, however, I knew that to be an effective reader and writer, a person needs to be aware of spelling. Knowing patterns and rules does help to decode words and to make connections between letters and sounds that then lead to fluency in reading and writing.

Then I bought a book on teaching spelling, and my biggest "aha!" was that spelling is developmental. The book contained lists for each grade level, and teachers could determine a child's developmental stage by how they spelled the words. I found it so interesting that how a child spelled a word could determine their developmental stage and influence what and how I taught those children. This screening tool was really quite accurate and helped me to understand what level students were at and how I could help them get to the next level.

After that, the way I taught spelling changed in my classroom. We used manipulatives, looked at patterns, and played with words. One of my favorite memories from first grade is when we were thinking of words that ended with *-ar*. I would give a clue, and students had to spell the word with their magnetic letters or write it on their whiteboard. For example, I said, "This is something you can ride in," and students excitedly spelled out "car." After spelling "far" and "star" and "war," I asked students if they had a riddle for a word that ended with *-ar*. I called on a student, and she whispered a word in my ear. "Okay," I said, all the while wondering what her riddle would be. "This is a place where daddies go after a hard day at work," she proudly shared. The students had no problem spelling out "bar," and here I was, thinking of "bar of soap" or "gold bar."

It was those kinds of activities that made a difference for my students. They began to look forward to the short spelling lessons, and for homework they made lists of words with the pattern we were learning. Students were delighted when they contributed a word to the list that other students might not have thought of. Students corrected spelling words in a paragraph or did other fun activities based on the pattern we were studying that week. We also had a word wall, and students had their own personal spelling handbook. They didn't have to worry about spelling for their first writing draft but they knew that self-correcting their spelling was part of the writing process, and they had tools they could rely on if they needed help.

Oh, one more thing: We did take spelling tests, but now, they weren't taken every Friday. Sometime during the week when I thought the students had internalized that spelling pattern, I assessed them, and I added in some bonus words for those who wanted a challenge. The students almost always spelled the words correctly, and if they made an error, they were able to self-correct their mistake. Most importantly, though, their subsequent writing assignments reflected that they had truly learned the spelling patterns of the words we had studied.

In this age of spell-check, is it important for students to learn to spell correctly? Yes, I believe that spelling still has a place in the classroom. Being an effective communicator and a quality producer means that the reader's understanding and enjoyment of a piece of writing is not hindered by poor spelling. How we teach spelling, however, does not have to be mundane or boring.

Why Can't I Be More Creative?
July 4, 2015

I remember reading a poem when I was in college titled "The Little Boy,"[5] by Helen Buckley, and it really impacted me as a teacher and as a mom. When I was an administrator, I remember watching Sir Ken Robinson's TED Talk, "Do schools kill creativity?"[6] That video impacted me as well, and I shared it with our teachers. Yet, I hid the fact that I was not confident whenever there was an activity that required me to be creative.

This was a hard blog post for me to write back in 2015, and it's still a bit uncomfortable rereading it today. I asked myself the same question many times—Why can't I be more creative?— but I really didn't want to admit it publicly. This blog post took longer for me to complete, but after I shared it with our staff, I felt like a weight had been lifted from my shoulders.

Schools need to explore creative ways to ensure that every student and every staff member has the tools they need to be successful. I may lack confidence in my own creativity, but I could still ensure that our students and our staff have those opportunities.

I'll be honest. I have no confidence in my creativity. I don't know why, but somewhere in my past I must have been told that I was not creative. So now, I have a difficult time being in a room with others and having an assignment to "create" something. I get that uncomfortable feeling and find myself watching and trying to hide the fact that I'm not actively participating or following instructions.

I think I was pretty good at getting my students to think creatively when I was a classroom teacher. I remember some of the fun activities we did, the many creative ideas my students came up with, and their confidence when sharing something original—an idea or a product. As a mom, I was determined that my sons would feel comfortable about thinking outside of the box, and I challenged them to make up their own games or to find creative uses for ordinary items. I made it a point to not buy coloring books but to have lots of paper, crayons, and pens around so they could draw what they wanted to and not have to "stay in the lines." My intentions were tested when my oldest went to kindergarten. The teacher shared that he had done well on the pretest but he could use help with his fine motor coordination. She then showed me all the other students' coloring of a bird and then showed me my son's. He had used an assortment of crayons and it wasn't neat like the others. When I asked my son about it, he proudly stated, "Everybody else used only one color. Mine was a rainbow bird; I used lots of colors!" As the year went by, I noticed that my son began to conform to what was expected. Did school kill his creativity?

What does it mean to be creative in school? What does that look like, and how do we get students to a place where thinking of and sharing creative ideas is the norm and not the exception?

So often in school, we structure our day so there is minimal time for students to explore, discover, and create on their own or with peers who have similar interests. The adult in the classroom tells students what to do, how to do it, and how much time they have to complete it. Activities such as writing or art, which are opportunities to share our creative ideas, are often structured as well, and we give students samples to follow or everyone is given the same assignment and is expected to complete it the same way. How do we move away from giving students the structure or the expectation to providing them with opportunities to think and act creatively? After much thought, here are my suggestions:

- We need to know our students, especially their interests and their strengths. Give them time to explore so they can discover what they enjoy doing or what they're good at.

Doing so can instill in them a confidence that they can contribute to their classroom community.
- Expose our students to great works of art, music, and literature from different cultures. They need to hear and see examples of the classics and to create their own ideas about why these have survived the test of time.
- Allow students to share their opinions and to understand that everyone is entitled to their own likes and dislikes based on their own personal experiences. Everyone's voice must be respected.
- Provide a structure for students where they brainstorm and think of as many ideas as they can. From this open-ended, divergent thinking activity, students choose one to focus on. For example, ask students to list as many uses as they can for a paper bag or a pencil or an envelope. Then students choose one unique idea, sketch out their process, and then create and share it. We may be surprised with the creative ideas that emerge from this simple activity.
- Model and share examples of creativity. Read a variety of literature, explore different art and music forms, share student examples as well to build an understanding of what creative thinking can be. The more we do this as teachers, the more natural it becomes.
- Give students different tools—both low-tech and high-tech—so they have a choice in how they want to create and share what they learn. Choice is a powerful motivator, and we might be pleasantly surprised at the final products. I was amazed with what some of our fifth graders created and shared when they could choose their own topic based on the theme of the quarter. Some students used tools that they discovered and learned to use on their own; clearly, the teacher had created a learning culture in her classroom where students were confident and self-directed learners.

- Finally, TIME is such an important factor if we want our students to be creative. Every student is different; some will jump right in, while others need time to reflect and think before coming up with an idea. We need to recognize these differences and make sure our schedule includes time for personalized learning.

So back to me and my lack of confidence when asked to create something. I realize that I may never overcome my discomfort when producing an art project. However, I can be creative in other ways, most importantly as a school leader. How we address the needs of our school community to ensure success takes commitment and creativity. I am committed, and I will continue to explore creative ways to ensure that every student and every staff member has the tools they need to be successful.

FINDING SOLUTIONS TO PROBLEMS
March 21, 2016

When I wrote this blog post in March 2016, I had made a decision to support our teachers to make the transition from interdisciplinary units (IDU) to project-based learning (PBL). With the right amount of professional development and guidance, I felt comfortable that we could do it. A few teachers were already dabbling in PBL, but we wanted to make this a school-wide goal because we believed it would help our students to demonstrate the skills of a successful and passionate learner and community contributor.

Our teachers received training in the different components of PBL, and we encouraged them to take small steps, to explore and try PBL strategies in their classrooms. A cohort of teacher volunteers received additional training that culminated in a showcase where students shared what they had learned with the school community. As a principal, I could not have been prouder of our students and teachers!

Today, many young people are choosing to make a difference outside of school. They realize that there are many who are struggling, and they have committed to helping them. When schools can give students the tools and inspire them via project-based learning, our society will be the beneficiary. As a principal, my goal was to prepare our students to ask questions, to find a passion and to pursue it, to make a difference in their own lives and in the lives of others. Transitioning from IDUs to PBL was an important part of that process.

This is spring break for us, a time to reflect on the past three quarters and look forward to our final quarter of the school year. This year, our tech team is leading our faculty in discussions about project-based learning. We realize that PBL is a mind shift from teacher-directed interdisciplinary units to being more student-directed, based on questions that are generated from the students themselves, and it has not been an easy transition.

As I walked around the school today, I stopped to admire the vegetables and plants that the second graders and the fifth grade garden club are growing. Then I noticed that the vines from the gourd plant were entwined on the native hibiscus plant. Last year, some fourth graders planted seeds from the gourds that they cleaned out, sanded, and polished to make *ipu*, a Hawaiian rhythm instrument. With minimal care, the gourd vines continue to grow. As our student services coordinator and I carefully disentangled the vines from the hibiscus bush, I made a lot of observations about how the vine was growing. I realized that this would be a perfect opportunity for students to ask questions about the plant and how it grows. This could lead to researching about the gourd plant and why it was so important to the ancient Hawaiians. Hopefully, when students make music with their ipu, they will have a better understanding and a better appreciation for the gourd.

Due to the construction on our campus, we have limited space for our students to play at recess. It's not too late to have our students be part of the solution. Let them have a discussion about what could be allowed at recess, what rules or restrictions we might have, and what new activities we might allow students to participate in during this free time. Why haven't we thought to ask them for their ideas? Students might be more invested in finding solutions to problems if we give them the opportunity to share in the discussion. After all, recess is essential for children.

Recently, a question was raised about a homework policy at our school. We've had this discussion before, but there was no consensus, so we decided that each grade level would determine its own policy. This time, our discussion was fueled by a blog about an elementary school that abolished homework. Since we are looking for opportunities to learn more about project-based learning, I think this is a perfect time to use a real-life problem and have all our role groups—teachers, students, and parents—contribute to the solution. We will come up with questions, then allow time for exploration, examining other schools' homework policies, sharing research about the benefits of homework, and discussing our findings. Hopefully, every role group's voices will be heard, and we will come up with some shared beliefs about homework that will help us create a policy for our school.

These kinds of discussions will help our teachers to gain a better understanding about the positive benefits of project-based learning. We can then empower our students to be problem finders and problem solvers, to seek solutions to everyday problems they may encounter in their lives.

LEARNING TO READ OR LOVING TO READ?
March 24, 2018

I believe strongly in the importance of literacy. When I started my career working with disadvantaged preschoolers and went on home visits to my students' homes, I noticed that often there were no books or other reading material around. When these students came to school, they had no idea what a book was or which way to turn the pages. For this reason, reading, writing, speaking, and listening skills were emphasized in my classroom, and by the end of the year, all students loved listening to stories and were borrowing books from our classroom library so parents could read to them at home.

I believe that we learn to read when we are ready. A few disadvantaged preschoolers in my Head Start class started school already decoding and reading simple books; obviously, they had reading material around their homes and had been read to. Sometimes, older students in elementary school struggled with decoding, but they loved being read to, remembered details, and had great insight after listening to a book. Not all students learn to read at the same age; some may need more time to make sense of the reading process.

I loved to read, and that is one reason why I chose to major in early childhood education. I wanted to share that love for literacy with my students. So often, teachers view reading and writing as subjects to teach in school. I prefer to think that reading, writing, speaking, and listening are essential skills for an informed citizenry. Life's Literacy Lessons[7] *really helped to validate my own thoughts. I'm glad I found this book and read it; it validated many of my ideas about reading instruction.*

It's the last weekend of spring break. I love these breaks because they afford me an opportunity to catch up on my reading—not just for professional growth but for enjoyment as well.

I don't know when I bought *Life's Literacy Lessons,* but I found it this week in a stack of books at home. (Spring break is also a great time to do some spring cleaning.) I loved that Steven L. Layne shared his views on reading instruction in humorous, nostalgic, and sometimes blunt anecdotes and poems. I found myself nodding my head, smiling to myself, and basically agreeing with the author's message.

When I began teaching reading many moons ago, I wasn't aware of all the scientific research behind reading. I was not on either side of the reading wars, and for some reason, I missed the political debate over the best way to teach reading. *The Reading Wars*[8] explains the controversy. For much of that time, I was teaching Head Start, and

I was shielded from that debate (thankfully). Teaching preschoolers who were from low-income families gave me the experiences I needed to understand that hands-on learning was crucial to help students make connections. When I became a teacher in elementary school, I was lucky. The principals I worked for weren't micromanagers, so I was able to teach reading using a variety of strategies; after all, our students were all different, at different levels, and with different interests.

Here are few of my beliefs about reading, gleaned after over 45 years as an educator:

- Reading instruction is not one-size-fits-all. Everyone is different, and what might work for one student might not work for another. As Steven L. Layne shares in his poem "For the Balanced Instruction Advocate" (page 14), "Balance is a difficult state to achieve. It takes dedication, perseverance and equal support from all sides. Teachers come equipped with these first two qualities. Why doesn't everyone just stop bickering and help us out with that last part."
- Students need to be surrounded by a variety of reading materials. We learn to read so we can read to learn. There are those who say that students in grades K–2 are learning to read so they can read to learn later. That is why the reading curriculum is heavy on phonics instruction in the early years. I don't buy that. Kids can learn from the time they are exposed to books and other reading material, and if their interest level is high, they just might surprise you with their knowledge.
- We need to make time every day to read aloud to students. Truthfully, reading aloud to my students was one of my favorite times of the day. I loved holding my kids captive with a great story. In his poem "Priorities" (page 62), Dr. Layne shares that, "It is easy to become convinced that

there are more important things to do than read to the kids. I really doubt it." I agree.
- I don't believe in inundating students with homework, but reading every day should be an expectation. It should be something the student has chosen to read, not something that is assigned based on Lexile levels or to complete a book report.
- As the mother and grandmother of boys, I am concerned that many of our boys are turned off to reading because we don't always allow them to read what they want to. I am reminded of a conversation with our school librarian last school year. Some of the kindergarten boys were in a section of the library that was "off-limits" for younger students. Our librarian shared that she needed to rethink the rules in the library. Why couldn't kindergarten boys borrow books about football if that's what they wanted? Let's not force our boys to read what we think they need and let them choose their reading material.
- I am not a fan of grade level standards for reading. Students come in at different places as far as reading is concerned. Expecting every student to achieve grade level standards does not take student differences into consideration. I would prefer using a continuum and starting where the child is and then planning next steps in the progression.
- There is no reason why we can't use available technology to help our students who need the most help with decoding and fluency. In this article, "The Goal of Phonics Instruction is to Get Readers Not to Use Phonics When Reading,"[9] the author shares two strategies that have been successful in producing gains in reading fluency and comprehension: assisted reading (listening to a text simultaneously while reading the text) and repeated reading (practicing several times until the reader can

read the text fluently). Students can independently use technology to help them self-assess their decoding and fluency. They can listen to another person reading the text while following along; they can time themselves to see how many words they can read in a minute, practice reading the same passage a few times and time themselves again to see their progress. We should teach students these strategies to help them become more fluent readers, which will lead to automaticity and hopefully, better comprehension.

- My final thought—when I read *Life's Literacy Lessons*, "Aliteracy Poem" hit home for me. One of the reasons I went into education was because I wanted students to realize their potential and to realize that we can learn something new every day of our lives. Reading is essential if we want to be lifelong learners. Dr. Layne (page 16) states, "Aliterate individuals are those who can read but choose not to do so. I often ask my graduate students, 'If we teach the children how to read, but none of them want to, have we done our jobs?'" I recently asked a 10-year-old who read voraciously when he was younger what he was reading. "Nothing," he replied. "I read in school, but that's it." It puzzled me. When this boy was seven, he asked for the set of the Diary of a Wimpy Kid books for his birthday and finished reading all of them within a month. What happened to his love of reading? Sometimes in our zeal to get our students to be better readers, we tell them what to read based on their reading level. But if students don't have the life experiences to relate to a book, they won't find that book enjoyable. Let them choose what to read.

So here I am on this dreary last weekend of spring break. Now that I've finished this blog post, I think I'll go read a book.

How Do We Teach History to Today's Kids?
June 23, 2019

I wrote this blog in June 2019 after we returned from our Revolutionary War/Civil War tour with our grandsons, who were nine and 12 years old at the time. It was an amazing experience to view history through their eyes, and it made me realize that what I learned when I was in school was mostly facts and memorization.

We are living in challenging times, and with the availability of news stations as well as social media, our children are experiencing history firsthand. COVID-19 has changed our lives, political discord is tearing our nation apart, and we have a nation that is far from unified. Educators are in a position to support our students to ask questions, to have tough discussions, to delve deeper into topics and being open to understand different points of view, and to be able to listen with empathy when others do not agree with us.

It is said that history repeats itself. If we don't want to make the same mistakes that we made in the past, we need informed and involved citizens. It starts in our schools.

When I was in school, history was taught through books and lectures. I learned names, dates, places, and events, but now, many years later, those details escape me. As we were preparing for our recent travels with our grandsons, I realized how little I actually knew aside from the basic facts. I realized that visiting those places as part of our travels with our grandsons this summer would be as much a learning experience for me as it was for them. It was eye- and mind-opening to walk the Freedom Trail, to learn more about the Salem witch trials, to interact with content at the various museums, or to stand on the grounds of the Gettysburg battlefields. I hope that our grandsons will remember their travels when they continue to learn in school about the history of our country.

Social studies—like science, math, language arts, physical education, and the arts—is essential in a school's curriculum. Social studies standards for our youngest students focus on a sense of self, then on their family and their community and working outward to their state, nation, and then the world. Within social studies, though, the National Council for Social Studies framework organizes the standards into ten themes such as culture, global connections, and civic ideals and practices. It can be overwhelming to find the time to address these standards, especially for an elementary teacher with many conflicting priorities during the day.

Oftentimes, as well, we view history through a single lens. Teaching history is complicated. There is more than one perspective to issues, and we don't know how the events impacted the people who were living during that period of time. Our grandsons realized that not all colonists wanted to fight the British. They also realized the sacrifices and impact of war on people, ordinary families whose lives were suddenly disrupted by events over which they had no control, people like the Shriver family, who lived in Gettysburg, or family members who fought on opposite sides during the Civil War.

We cannot change history; it is in the past. We can educate ourselves and learn what others went through at the time by visiting museums, reading books, or watching videos, but we cannot experience what the people went through. When we discuss history, let's start with deeper questions and research to find answers and then discuss why the events unfolded as they did. We need to understand the impact of events on the people who were affected and discuss how those events impact us today.

And we must vow to learn from the mistakes of our past. Unfortunately, I am not confident that we have done so. There was a wall at the Salem Witch Museum with the words, "Fear + Trigger = Scapegoat." How many examples can we think of from our country's history that had its beginnings in fear? Is it still happening today? Why is it important to not repeat our mistakes from the past?

I know that our recent travel experiences to Boston, Philadelphia, and Washington, DC, have made me think much more deeply about our country's history. I realize that if our forefathers had not had the courage to break away from Britain and fight to create a new nation, our own history would be much different than it is today.

Make Time for Writing
November 29, 2020

I think that nothing pleased me more as a teacher of young children than to see the progress my students made in writing. At the beginning of the year, many were writing random strings of letters, and by the time they left our classroom, they were writing stories and books. I loved that students often chose to write when they had free time.

For some students, writing words and sentences was a struggle, but they could draw a picture, write a sentence, and add details as I wrote down what they dictated to me. It was my hope that my students would continue to share their thoughts and ideas through writing and that they would see it as a desirable activity, something they enjoyed.

When I started blogging back in 2012, I found that it helped me to organize and share my thoughts and opinions, mostly about education. At the outset, I had no idea how long I would continue blogging, but I'm still at it today.

After I retired and our son Jarand passed away unexpectedly, writing helped to quiet my mind. It was therapy for me to sit and remember and reflect. Jarand was my inspiration to continue writing. I wrote this in late 2020 as I was selecting which blog posts to include in this book.

As I look back at all my past blog points, I realized that I had not shared my thoughts about writing even though I believe it is one of the best ways for students to take their thinking to a higher level. I observed younger students who were eager to write and share their stories with others. Then somewhere in their educational journey, students lost their interest to write. I think it happened at around third grade, when the focus became high-stakes testing and students were taught to follow certain steps to respond to writing prompts. I saw so many student samples that looked and sounded similar.

They started the same way by turning the question posed into their introductory and concluding statements. "Do you think dogs make better pets than cats? Why?" became "I think dogs make better pets than cats because first . . . ." Then they proceeded to name three reasons and concluded with "That's why dogs make better pets than cats." It worked for standardized tests but not as a way to measure creative writing.

When I started blogging, I realized how challenging it was to actually write and publish something for anyone to read. Yet our youngest students never felt that way. They were proud to share and to have others comment or even to offer suggestions for improvement. They were able to revise and to write a final copy that was a marked improvement over their first draft. They were thrilled when the teacher chose to post their writing on the walls for others to see. I think back to my school days, and I don't think I ever shared my writing with anyone other than the teacher.

I was newly retired when I wrote my book *Leading with Aloha: From the Pineapple Fields to the Principal's Office* and I realized how challenging writing is. After many hours, drafts, edits, suggestions from others, and lots of soul-searching about whether this was something I really wanted, I persevered, and I'm glad I did. I wish I could share that experience with students today.

As I worked on a web page to promote and advertise my book, I shared some of my thoughts about teaching writing.

- If children can think, they can say what they're thinking. If they can say it, they can write it. Their "writing" may be scribbles, but encourage them to tell you what they wrote. Write it down and read it back to them. This is the first connection children make between thinking, speaking, writing, and reading.
- Just as we realize the importance of reading in our instruction, we need to understand the importance of writing.

- Make time for children to write. There is no need to provide a prompt. Young kids have so many creative ideas of their own.
- Not all students will be at the same developmental writing stage. Start where they are and build on their skills. Point out to students how they're improving. Help them set goals to improve their writing.
- Writing is hard work for children. Build children's stamina for writing by gradually lengthening the time allocated for writing. Make sure students are writing during this time.
- Encourage students to add to their stories and praise their effort.
- Even students as young as kindergarten can help with peer editing. Model how to ask questions for clarification. Ensure that students have opportunities to revise or edit their writing.
- Introduce students to different kinds of writing: fiction, nonfiction, poetry, plays, letters. There are so many ways to express what we've learned as well as our thoughts and feelings.
- All students can self-edit when coached through the process. Instead of telling students what they need to improve, ask open-ended questions so students can reflect and make revisions that work for them.
- Share and celebrate student writing with an authentic audience, if possible. Students will have more pride in doing their best writing when they know it will be shared with more than just their teacher or classmates.

One of the initiatives we were working on at our school before I retired was creating and using a continuum for narrative writing with our students. We hoped to use this tool so our students would be able to self-assess where they are, how they could edit and improve on what they wrote, and how they could set goals or next steps. With the pandemic and the need for teachers to learn new skills and strategies via virtual learning, I think the writing continuum initiative has probably been put on the back burner for now. Hopefully, though, teachers have seen this pandemic as an opportunity for students to document their feelings and experiences during this challenging time. Whether they do it through writing or some other means, we need to provide time for our students to share their thoughts and ideas. Maybe one day, they will be able to look back and reflect on how the pandemic impacted their lives and they can share these experiences with their grandchildren. "The year was 2020 . . ."

SELF-REFLECTION AND GOAL SETTING
November 30, 2020

During the pandemic, when most schools were instructing virtually, I read educators' questions and comments on social media, and one topic was about grading. How do we test students or give report card grades during a pandemic?

I decided to write this blog post because I think it's time to reexamine how we grade students. As someone who strived for good grades when I was a student, I realize that this is quite a turnaround in my attitude towards grades. I've asked myself these questions: What is the purpose of grades and who are they for? If we believe that students are the most important person in the learning cycle, why are they not part of the grading process? Does a higher grade point average mean a person will be more successful in life? How do we get students to be more invested in their learning without using grades as a motivator? Self-reflection and goal setting might be the answer.

I remember the first time I sat in on a student-led conference. Our youngest son, Jordan, was in the fifth grade, and it was conference week. We received a letter from the teacher informing us that students would be leading their conference. The big day came;

our son was a bit nervous when he began, but his voice grew stronger as he shared several pieces of work that he was proud of. They were assignments he had worked on in class. One was for the book they were reading, and it was a diary with illustrations and entries from the main character's point of view; another was a math problem-solving assignment where he had to show his work and explain his thinking, and the third was an art project. He also shared a couple of assignments where he felt he could have improved his effort, and he shared what his goals were for the remainder of the year. In subsequent quarters, our son's report card included a self-assessment with new evidences of learning as well as his reflections on how he was doing on his goals. I was so impressed, and when I became a principal, I hoped we could include students in their own conferences. Several teachers decided to try it out with great success, and after hearing from these teachers, student-led conferences became part of the culture at our school.

Students as young as preschool were able to sit in on a conference and share some of their work with their parents. In the process, they were able to work on their communication skills, something that many of those preschoolers had difficulty with. Our teachers had flexibility on how they used the time allocated for conference week. Some chose to schedule 20-minute blocks of time for each student and his/her family. Others had several families come in for a longer time period, and the teacher rotated to each group while students shared their portfolio of work with their parents. Other teachers scheduled two families for 40-minute blocks; students were able to "walk the room" for half the time with their parents, sharing the different activities in each area while the teacher sat with the other family and guided students as they shared their work and reflections with their parents. Walking around during these conferences was a proud moment for me as a principal. Parents were beaming with pride, some with tears in their eyes. We realized how empowering these conferences were for their children. These student-led conferences showed us that it is the learner who is most important in school, and it is the learner whose voice needs to be heard.

Report card grades or a student's score on a standardized test don't necessarily tell us about what the child has learned or what the child is interested in. Reflections, sharing self-selected work, and goal setting ensures that the student, the parent, and the teacher are invested in helping the child make progress towards their goals. We want our students to be self-directed learners and to set goals for themselves, and to know that the teacher and the parent are there to support them. That three-way partnership goes a long way to ensuring success for the student.

Explore, Discover, Create, and Share
Reflective Questions

- Think back to your education training. What did you learn about teaching and learning that are still important to you today?
- In today's rapidly changing world, how do we balance teaching required skills and knowledge with innovative practices?
- Reflect on a unit or a lesson in your classroom that engaged and empowered students in their own learning. What made it successful? What would you change?
- The four C's of 21st-century learning are collaboration, communication, critical thinking, and creating. We can also add a fifth C—choice. How do you integrate 21st-century teaching and learning strategies in your classroom?
- How can we create time to ensure that students have the opportunity to pursue something they are passionate about during the school day?
- Describe an innovative idea that you implemented in your classroom or at your school.
- How can today's educational system better prepare our students for the world they will be leading in the future?

- Think about your classroom or your school. How might you make little changes that could have a big impact on students?
- How do your students reflect on their learning? How has this helped them to be more responsible and self-directed learners?
- Referencing John W. Gardner's quote at the beginning of this chapter, how often do you allow students to grow their own plants? How might you provide more time for growing plants rather than giving them cut flowers? ♥

NOTES

CHAPTER FOUR

Build Teacher Capacity

"The most important thing is to try and inspire people
so that they can be great in whatever they want to do."
—*Kobe Bryant*

Teachers are essential to the future of our state, our nation, and our world. I have worked with and supervised hundreds of teachers, and I know they were committed to making a difference for their students. For them, teaching was a calling, not just a job. They cared about their students. They worked long hours to plan lessons that would help their students to progress, and they did their best to be good soldiers, to do what was expected from their school, their district, and their state. The truth is that often our teachers and our administrators are overwhelmed with so many responsibilities and expectations. This was especially evident during the recent pandemic, when schools were suddenly confronted with changing from face-to-face, in-person learning to distance learning. Schools realized the need to change, but the learning curve was steep, not just for teachers, but for students as well. Teachers were exhausted.

A positive relationship and trust between an administrator and the teacher can make a huge difference. When a teacher is hired, the principal's job is to help that person be confident and reflective, continually seeking to improve his/her practice. This is a team effort with the school community providing support and assistance. It doesn't happen overnight, and there is no magic formula to becoming a great teacher; in fact, even our best teachers know that they have room for improvement. Teachers need to have more than book knowledge. They need to care; be willing to build positive, trusting relationships; and work with their colleagues to continuously improve to be their best for their students.

Our world is changing, and the skills our students need to be successful in the future are far different today. We need innovative, creative teachers who are able to motivate their students to ask questions and search for answers. We need teachers who are able to guide students to understand how to apply the skills they learn in class to real-life problems. We need teachers who understand that every child is different, and we need to be flexible with our curriculum in order to address each child's individual interests, strengths, and challenges.

The most effective teachers are continually learning and striving to improve. They review data and adjust lessons based on the strengths, needs, and interests of their students. They network and collaborate with others to share research or best practices. They provide honest feedback and conference with their students so they can continue their journey as learners. They seek opportunities to grow professionally and engage their students in meaningful work that will help them in the future, not just in school, but in life. Students of the most effective teachers are confident learners who are willing to take risks, make mistakes, and learn from them.

Do teachers need to be observed by an administrator? Should students be learning in the classroom? Should the classroom be well managed? Should students like their teacher? Should we have expectations for teachers? The answer is yes to all of these questions. However, it's the how that needs to be clarified.

As a principal, my worth to the school is lessened when much of my time is spent on required tasks that tell me what I already know. I know which teachers are doing well and which teachers are struggling. I know when a class is particularly challenging and which teachers need more support and affirmations. I know which teachers are reaching out to ask for help and which ones are hesitant to admit that they are struggling with a few difficult students. Rather than spending my time documenting that I met with teachers to complete Department-directed required tasks, I would have preferred to have more opportunities for unplanned observations or meetings or to have informal conversations with teachers about successes or challenges in their classrooms. A trusting relationship between students and their teacher and between teachers and their administrator can lead to risk-taking, confidence, and learning from failures as well as successes.

This is what education should be: empowering principals to empower teachers to empower students. Education is about leadership to innovate and to create. Our students will be better prepared for life if we empower our teachers and our students to take responsibility for their own learning.

In this chapter, I discuss different ways we guided and supported teachers at our school so they could be the best they could be for their students. Every teacher is different with different strengths and challenges; we built on that diversity to create a community of teacher learners with the capacity to continue to grow their profession.

Textbooks or Professional Development for Teachers?
September 3, 2012

I wrote this post in 2012 as our teachers were transitioning from the Hawaiʻi Content Performance Standards (HCPS) to the Common Core State Standards (CCSS) that had been adopted by almost every state. At the time, I mistakenly hoped that if we had common standards throughout our country, our transient military students would not have gaps when they enrolled at our school. I bought the idea that we would be comparing apples to apples instead of apples to oranges regarding curriculum, teaching, and learning.

I was wrong. I think for many schools, districts, or states, adopting the CCSS meant purchasing a curriculum that supposedly aligned to the new standards. In this blog post, I shared that rather than spending money on textbooks that could be outdated in a few years, it would be better to invest in our teachers, to help them make sense of the standards and to create engaging lessons and assessments.

Our school is struggling to provide the necessary professional development for teachers to implement the Common Core State Standards (CCSS). It takes much more than reviewing our old curriculum and aligning our lessons to the CCSS. The expectations for teaching and learning are much higher now, and making the change at the school level, in every classroom, is a challenge. Understanding the CCSS takes time, honest discussion, modeling, reflection, and collaborating with our colleagues. We had few opportunities to have deep discussions with the entire faculty to address the individual needs of our school and our students to meaningfully implement the new standards.

Presently, publishing companies are aligning their textbooks, and states, districts, and schools will soon be reviewing these resource materials to select one that aligns with the CCSS and best fits their needs. However, rather than spending millions of dollars on new textbooks, perhaps we should invest in our teachers by providing planning and collaboration time so they can create relevant, problem-based or project-based learning opportunities that integrate the CCSS as well as the use of technology and other resources. There are so many resources available for accessing curriculum as well as for sharing learning, but it takes the competency and the creativity of the teacher to make learning come alive for students.

A few years ago, Dr. Julia Myers trained our teachers on Lesson Study for math. Lesson Study was developed in Japan and builds the capacity of teachers to learn from each other and to observe student learning in the classroom. The process was powerful. Through

Lesson Study, our teachers became better observers of students and worked together to design problem-based math lessons and conduct action research focused on a school-wide goal. However, there were obstacles to full implementation, primarily the cost of hiring substitutes so teachers could collaborate to develop their Lesson Study plans and ensuring coverage for classrooms so that teachers could observe each other, debrief, and revise their lesson afterwards. This is not a problem in Japan, where teachers spend 60% of their time teaching and 40% meeting with other teachers to collaborate, plan, and receive professional guidance from mentors. It was a problem for us.

In this, the Information Age, students need to learn more than content; they need to learn how to think and how to process information and share their ideas. Grade level standards and statewide assessments should not be the whole focus. If we want our students to be self-directed and independent learners, community-minded citizens, and complex and creative thinkers and problem solvers, we should be focusing on professional development for teachers rather than purchasing costly textbooks that may quickly outlive their usefulness. Teachers want to learn and improve their craft, but very little time is allocated during the school day or week to collaborate with colleagues, to observe teaching and learning in other classrooms, to analyze student work, and to reflect to improve their practices.

The CCSS has the potential to change the way teaching and learning takes place in schools. However, real change will only come about when teachers have the competency to be creators of the curriculum in their classrooms and to plan relevant and engaging learning opportunities based on the strengths, needs, and interests of their students. To accomplish this, rather than spending millions on new textbooks, we should consider spending more on supporting our teachers through guided professional development and time to collaborate and learn from others. Only then will we see meaningful changes in schools.

CHALLENGING TIMES FOR EDUCATORS
February 1, 2014

I believe in the power of schools to change the lives of students and their families. Unfortunately, many in the public have been critical of our schools, and educators often endure unfair criticism, all the while doing their best for their students. Schools face similar problems, whether they are in Hawai'i or in other parts of our country—problems such as lack of adequate funding, teacher shortages, too many responsibilities added to the plate with nothing taken off, and criticism from the public about not preparing students adequately.

The year 2014 happened to be the last year of our state's Race to the Top grant from the federal government, and we had to show evidence that all of the requirements had been met. I know all of us principals breathed a sigh of relief when the grant was over. Fortunately, DOE asked for feedback and modified many of the expectations for schools so we could focus on what was important for teaching and learning at our schools.

I have been an educator for over forty years. I began as a Head Start teacher where I worked with low-income preschoolers and their parents. My core beliefs about education were validated and strengthened during my early teaching years. We took care of students and their families—feeding and teaching them about nutritious meals and the importance of medical and dental care, helping families to access health or social service resources, encouraging parents to volunteer in the classroom so they would know how to interact and converse with their children. These early teaching experiences convinced me of the need to care for our students and their families so they could be successful in school and in life. Throughout my years as a teacher and an administrator, my philosophy of teaching and learning has changed very little: I believe in the power of schools to change the lives of our students and their families.

These are challenging times for educators in our state and around the nation. It seems that everyone has an opinion about what is wrong with our schools, and educators endure unfair criticism, all the while doing their best to help students learn.

So, here are my random personal thoughts about how we might improve education.

- A well-rounded curriculum includes time for students to be exposed to more than just the academic subjects. When student test scores or student growth is the priority, non-tested subjects may get pushed to the side. Every student should have opportunities to be exposed to experiences with the arts, physical education, or other subjects. Teachers, too, should have the opportunity to teach to their strengths and interests. When teachers are excited about what they're teaching, their students may be impacted by that enthusiasm.
- Teachers learn to design comprehensive lessons during their university coursework, but often, when they get to a school, they are expected to follow a scripted curriculum guide. Our teachers followed the grade level quarterly matrices, but they were able to create their own lessons to address the standards and the needs of their students. Teachers appreciated that we trusted them to do what was best for them as well as for their students.
- Our state is using an observation process as part of a teacher's evaluation. In a 180-day school year, two observations—about 1.5 hours total—will be used to evaluate performance. I agree that administrators need to be in classrooms, and teachers need to reflect on their teaching. However, formal observations should be an opportunity for discussions to improve teaching and learning, not as an evaluative tool.
- Teachers need more professional development time: time to collaborate, to visit other classrooms, to plan lessons together, and to learn from each other. Our system provides

limited opportunities for teachers to improve their practice. Improving teacher effectiveness will have a greater impact on student performance than evaluating teachers based on student test scores.
- And finally, way too much emphasis is placed on standardized tests. In the real world, we are judged by our performance on the job, not by a standardized test score. Let's rethink high-stakes testing and move towards performance-based assessments to evaluate student learning.

I agree that we need to improve education for our children and that schools and teachers need to be accountable for preparing students for their future. I hope that the public will trust that teachers have the expertise to positively impact teaching and learning. Schools need to know they are supported as they take on the challenge of educating our nation's greatest resource—our children.

Should Observations Be Part of a Teacher's Evaluation?
March 29, 2015

I was part of a pilot program for principals where we received training about the Danielson Framework. It was an extensive and exhaustive process to use all the components of the Framework to evaluate all teachers at our school, and I remember giving feedback that the process was too cumbersome. When the DOE rolled out the final teacher evaluation system, administrators were responsible for doing two evaluations on each teacher using criteria for five components of the Danielson Framework.

I wrote this blog post in March 2015, and in October of that year the Department of Education shared that in school year 2014-2015, 98% of Hawai'i public school teachers were rated Effective or Highly Effective, and the number of Highly Effective teachers went up from 1,846 (16%) in school year 2013–2014 to 4,206 (35%). I was not surprised by these results. I knew that we would have a much higher number of

Highly Effective" teachers, primarily because we had gone through the challenges the year before. Teachers knew what to expect and what they had to do to earn the Highly Effective designation. I recall that the Board of Education was concerned that perhaps the criteria was not rigorous enough, producing false returns.

In this blog post, I raise questions about how we were observing and evaluating teachers.

As a principal, I should be observing teachers and helping them to reflect on the strengths of the lesson as well as any challenges that can be areas for growth. The question is, Should a formal observation be part of the evaluation system? Should one observation be part of a teacher's yearlong rating?

I reflected on the teacher observations I've been doing every year since I became a principal. Here are some of my thoughts:

- A trusting relationship between the teacher and the administrator is essential. In such a relationship, the teacher will often come to the post-observation conference having already reflected on how they can improve the lesson in the future. One example of the trust a teacher had with me was when she shared that she was having difficulty with one of her students. She had hoped he would exhibit the challenging behaviors during the lesson so I could observe how she dealt with the student and possibly give her some suggestions or insights. This teacher viewed the observation as an opportunity to grow and improve in her practice, not just as a score on her evaluation.
- Visiting classrooms is the best part of my job, and spending time with students informs me about the teaching and learning taking place every day in the classroom, not just during a formal observation. The informal conversation afterward is one way for administrators to create a trusting relationship with the teacher. That relationship is essential

as we constantly strive to improve teaching and learning at our school.
- As teachers begin to blend their lessons with students using technology as an essential component of their learning, the evaluation tool we are using may not be useful as we observe what is going on in the classroom. The tool does not take into account that learning can happen virtually or collaboratively via technology. When teachers have to plan their lesson so an observer can collect a plethora of evidence to warrant a rating, it is less likely that a teacher will plan a virtual assignment where evidence may not be observable.
- Any formal observation by an administrator should be an opportunity for improvement rather than an evaluative tool. We want teachers to take risks and to be flexible when they are teaching. When teachers are given a rating that counts towards their evaluation, most of them will play it safe. We want teachers to be creative, to learn from imperfect lessons, and to reflect on what they might need to change to make them successful in the future.

The conversation prior to and after the observations are essential to building positive relationships with teachers. I wanted my teachers to trust me to be honest with them and to ask the tough questions to get them to think about their lessons. In the end, though, it is just one lesson for one hour of a whole school year. We should care more about what happens on the other 179 school days.

Proud of Our Teacher Presenters
April 20, 2015

I believe in social media for professional development. As a school leader, I realized the need to be connected to other educators—not just in Hawai'i but in other parts of the country—to learn from them, to validate what we were doing at our school, and to continue my profes-

sional growth.

Teachers in Hawai'i often do not get the opportunity to hear from nationally recognized speakers. Travel costs are high, and schools often lack the funds. When I heard via social media that Eric Sheninger was going to be speaking at a conference here on O'ahu, I wanted our teachers to have the opportunity to hear him. We encouraged our teachers to submit a request to be presenters so they could attend the conference without paying the registration fee. Several were accepted and prepared great presentations to share with colleagues from other schools. It was a win-win for these teachers who had the opportunity to hear Eric keynote the conference while gaining confidence as presenters.

Many teachers are doing amazing things with their students. It takes courage to step out of their comfortable classrooms and to share their successes with their colleagues. We need to encourage our teachers to share!

This past weekend, several of our teachers and I attended the Moanalua High School Professional Development Conference with keynoter Eric Sheninger. Last summer, Eric gave up part of his Hawai'i vacation to speak to educators from our DOE complex area, and he made quite an impression. This past week, Eric has been very busy, sharing about digital leadership not only at this conference but with teams from different complex areas on O'ahu and the Big Island.

But this blog is not about Eric; it's about our teachers and their willingness to share with others about what they have learned about the use of technology with students to explore, discover, create, and share. At this latest conference, our teachers shared about a wide range of topics—virtual coaching, Google Sites, Kinder Creations, Google Presentations, using social media to grow your professional learning network, and tools and tips for integrating technology. I was really proud of them all; it takes courage to step out of the box to share with strangers.

I believe that the strength of a school is in its staff and their willingness to try new ideas and share their successes and challenges.

Our teachers have presented at various conferences on a variety of different topics. Those who are hesitant have the opportunity to try presenting to their colleagues first at an afternoon Tech Tip Tuesday session or at a faculty meeting. Our teachers can build their confidence, and if they are afraid to go solo, we encourage them to partner with someone else. That usually works well.

It is rare for classroom teachers to have the opportunity to hear someone like Eric speak unless they attend a conference. Because they were presenters, our teachers' registration fees were waived. Eric's keynote validated that we are on the right path in creating a school—or classrooms—that works for students. It is about continuously learning. We need to prepare our students for the world they will live in. It is a work in progress, but Eric's keynote showed the teachers and other conference attendees that with their leadership, we can move forward in the right direction.

Support for New Teachers
July 10, 2016

"I was feeling sorry for myself. Here it was near the end of June, and we still hadn't completed our hiring for the next school year. For every teacher applicant who agreed to a meeting with us, there were 10 who had already been hired at another school or declined to interview (too far, no transportation, etc.).

This year, more than any other in my tenure at our school, we had a lot of staff leave. All were for good reasons—retirement, new assignment for their military spouse, beginning the journey to become an administrator, staying home with their new baby, or moving to a new school either here in Hawai'i or in a different state. No one left because they wanted to quit teaching." I wrote these words in June 2016.

Hiring new teachers can be challenging. I remember those days just before the start of school when we would be scrambling to hire teachers for positions that were suddenly vacant or that were recently created due to an increase in enrollment. As a statewide system, we had lists *with lots of names, but many of those teachers had already been hired at another school or they had moved or they didn't respond to the phone call or email. When I wrote this blog in July 2016, we had hired most of our teachers, and I was looking forward to working with all of them during the upcoming school year.*

This will be my 14th year as principal of our school, and the first that we have such a turnover of teachers. In my last blog, I shared my feelings about losing staff and hiring new teachers. I ended the blog on a positive note, and I feel confident that we will benefit from the individual strengths and life experiences of our new staff.

Since then, I read a timely and relevant blog, "8 Characteristics of a Great Teacher,"[10] and it was such validation of what I believe as an administrator. I reflected on our interviews with numerous applicants, and I know why we selected the teachers we did. When we ask our interview questions, we are listening to the candidates' core beliefs and their life experiences about why they went into teaching and what they can offer to our students and school community. We can tell when they are being honest and saying what they believe. Throughout the interview, woven into the different questions we ask, we get a glimpse into that teacher's philosophy and beliefs about education and about children. We were picky; even though we had a number of openings, we preferred to ask for another list if we didn't feel that anyone would be the kind of teacher who would thrive in our school.

Many of the teachers we hired are new to the state or new to the profession, and they bring a wealth of experiences to our school. I am excited about what they shared when we asked about any innovative projects they had been involved with. They are committed to building strong relationships with their students, especially those who are the most challenging. As the interview ended, some teachers found a way to add that they are not textbook- or worksheet-driven and prefer to engage students through inquiry-based, hands-on activities that encourage collaboration and communication with others. I was pleased that these interviewees were confident enough to let me know up front about their beliefs and practices. As part of our interview process, we want any teacher applicant to know that as a school, we believe that there is a general guideline of what students need to learn and do, but teachers are encouraged to use their own strengths as well as the strengths and interests of their students to provide a rich, engaging, and empowering classroom curriculum.

What these interviews indicated to me was contrary to what we've been hearing about schools today. The teachers we hired did not talk about high test scores or following a set program. They shared about knowing their kids and building a community within their classroom so their students would feel safe and will want to come to school even if they are experiencing challenges such as transitions or deployments. They are excited to try new things that we have implemented at our school like creating a class web page to communicate with families or using technology to share student learning. And they embraced our school vision, "Empowering learners to explore, discover, create, and share," and related our vision to themselves as teachers and learners.

Now that we have found the teachers we want for our school, it is our responsibility as administrators to provide them with the support and guidance they need to be successful in their new positions. Our grade level teams, instructional coaches, technology team, and mentor teachers are essential in providing that support. After all, teaching is a challenging profession, but with the right support, our new teachers will continue to grow personally and professionally.

Making Time for Teachers to Learn in PLCs
May 5, 2018

Early in my principalship, I decided to give our teachers an opportunity to work in groups to explore a topic they might be interested in as part of their personal professional development. Although some teachers liked this opportunity, others were critical, and I remember abandoning the idea the following year. When I reflected a few years later, I realized why this format was not as successful as I hoped it would be. The problem was that I had not given teachers any voice. I decided on the topics, and although teachers got to choose which group they wanted to join, there was little guidance about what were the expected outcomes.

As I learned more about student voice and choice in project-based learning (PBL), I realized that teachers also needed that opportunity, so I decided to give professional learning communities (PLCs) another try. This blog, written in May 2018, shared how we can use PBL processes with our teachers as well as our students.

We had our last project-based learning discussion with our staff last Wednesday so we could reflect on our past year and look forward to the new year ahead. Our final question was, "What do you need to move forward with PBL?"—because with the success of our showcase last month, the expectation is that *all* students will have these kinds of learning opportunities.

Teachers shared their ideas on Post-its, and our next step is to have grade level and resource teachers look over all the responses from their colleagues and come up with ideas on how to move forward. Rather than the PBL leadership team making decisions (top-down), we will be getting input and feedback from those who will be impacted. We want to hear about how best to address the needs of *all* teachers at *all* stages of PBL—those who were part of the cohort or are the "experts" (compared to their colleagues), those who have received training and are ready to give it a try, and those who are newbies who will probably need more support. I'm excited to see what ideas our teachers come up with.

This past year, we decided to give teachers time to explore a topic of their own choosing as part of our Wednesday meeting schedule. For want of a better descriptor, we called it professional learning communities (PLC). The first step was to ask teachers what they wanted to explore as part of their professional growth. We collected all the responses, categorized them, and had teachers select their top three choices. We then divided staff into manageable PLC groups. Groups were diverse. The number in each group varied, and different grade levels were represented. Teachers were able to work with those they might not usually collaborate with.

One of the most important assignments was to agree on a driving question that would answer the question, "Why are we doing this?" This would give the PLC focus on what to explore and discover. Examples of the driving questions they came up with:

- How can we impact student achievement through play?
- How can I as a teacher integrate technology in my classroom to support 21st-century learning?
- How can we create the best and most effective model for co-teaching at DKIES?
- Why do we want students to be empowered and how do we get them there?
- How can a focus on STEM (or STEAM) impact student achievement?
- How will learning and trying out new strategies improve student reading and writing achievement?

Teachers had opportunities to work individually or in a group. They shared ideas with each other and had rich conversations about what they learned. They collaborated to complete tasks and review resources that were then shared with the rest of the teachers through a shared presentation. We gave teachers time to review and comment on the other PLCs' slides. Most of the teachers used their PLC exploration as their Individualized Professional Development Plan (IPDP) for their yearly teacher evaluation. As we met with teachers for their end-of-the-year summary, administrators were having more meaningful and reflective discussions with teachers about their IPDP.

Our last PLC meeting this school year will be a showcase, an opportunity for teachers to share what they learned and tried out in their classrooms as well as any evidence of their personal learning in their PLCs. We believe that giving teachers opportunities to share and learn from their colleagues builds community and breaks down barriers within our school. With nearly 70 teachers spread out over a large campus, finding the time to share and learn from each other can be challenging.

Our teachers may not realize it, but they participated in their PLC using project-based learning processes, something we are transitioning to with our students. We started with a driving question, and they decided what they wanted to explore more deeply. They asked relevant questions and used 21st-century skills—collaboration, communication, critical thinking—to research and learn from each other. Teachers had voice and choice in what they wanted to explore and discover with their PLC, and they were learning from their colleagues. These led to discussions as well as validation of the direction the group was going in. Finally, there will be a publicly presented product, although it will be just within our school at this time.

As we reflected with teachers on their IPDP, they shared concerns with the PLC process. We believed it was an effective way for teachers to explore an area they wanted to know more about; however, only one extended PLC Wednesday meeting time per quarter meant that the learning process was not as effective as it could be. As one teacher reflected, "I was hoping that we could spend more time sharing and discussing ways to implement some of the things we researched. I felt like we spent more time researching and talking about what we were learning. We didn't give ourselves time to discuss what we could implement in class. And with the time in between, I don't think we remembered our previous discussions and often spent time looking at what we talked about."

I believe that professional development for teachers needs to be differentiated. Just as every student in a classroom has different strengths, needs, and interests, so do teachers at a school. We realize that time will always be a challenge, so we need to be more effective in the use of available time. By asking teachers for their reflections about how to improve the process, adjustments can be made to maximize the kind of collaboration that ultimately will positively impact student learning.

SHOULD OUR BEST AND BRIGHTEST BECOME TEACHERS?
January 10, 2019

I remember meeting a young man whom I hadn't seen since his high school graduation about 20 years previously. When I asked him what he was doing, he replied, "I'm just a teacher."

"What do you mean, just a teacher?" I asked.

"Well, most of my friends from high school are doctors or lawyers," he responded, as if he were embarrassed to be "just a teacher." I went into my lecture mode and told him to be proud of being a teacher. After all, without teachers, none of the other professions would be possible.

In June 2019, one of our former teachers, Kat Araujo, who started a business in New York, shared this on Instagram: "Teaching was equal parts creativity and administration, and it helped me build character, taught me resilience, and gave me solid leadership skills." She went on to say, "I haven't been in the classroom for over seven years now, but I am still benefiting from this experience. I learned a lot about managing others, and building a culture that brings out the best in people. I also gained the confidence to go after my dreams." I've been following this young female entrepreneur, and I am so proud of all that she is accomplishing.

This is perhaps one of the most important blog posts I have written because instead of discouraging our "best and brightest" from becoming teachers, we should be encouraging them. What better way for them to make a difference with our young people!

"How would you respond when someone you respect tells you your talents and abilities are being 'wasted' as a teacher?"

I saw this question posted on Twitter, and I've been thinking of an appropriate response. I know that the "best and brightest" are often encouraged to become attorneys or doctors or engineers and discouraged from going into teaching. How do we change the perception that teaching is not for our "best and brightest?"

Through my years as an educator, I worked with or connected with teachers who were in their second career. They worked in businesses or had jobs in the travel industry or were engineers out of college. Some of them took pay cuts to become teachers, and when questioned, their responses were similar. They shared that they didn't feel fulfilled in their previous profession and absolutely did not regret their decision to become teachers and to make a positive difference for the next generation.

What motivates us in our decision to pursue a career? Is it status? Economic stability? The ability to grow professionally? The opportunity to make a difference? Impacting our next generation? Something that stokes a passion? If we pursue a career for the "wrong" reasons, we may not feel fulfilled and may not give our best effort.

Not everyone can be a teacher. It takes a special kind of person to spend their whole day with kids and to commit to all the expectations of an educator. Teachers teach much more than academic skills. School is an opportunity for students to learn empathy, to work with others who have different strengths and challenges, to gain confidence through support from not just teachers but from classmates as well, to care about our world, to be exposed to new ideas, to have opportunities to pursue passions they didn't know about before, and so much more! Teachers don't just teach content. Teachers teach students, and therefore, teachers impact our future. These students will be our workforce, our leaders, our innovators to tackle the challenges in our community, our state, our country, and our world.

I can't think of a more influential profession than teaching. After all, every other profession depends on teachers to do their job in educating our children. Journalist Charles Kuralt stated, "When we become a mature, grown-up, wise society, we will put teachers at the center of the community, where they belong. We don't honor them enough; we don't pay them enough." Nelson Mandela shared, "Education is the most powerful weapon for changing the world."

I recently read this article by Valerie Strauss, a writer for the *Washington Post*, and teacher Julie Hiltz: "What teaching is and isn't."[11] I think they accurately and succinctly explain why others may think that the "best and brightest" should aspire to a different profession. As for me, I was thrilled to hire the "best and brightest" at our school. Giving them opportunities to grow professionally and to take on leadership roles made a difference for our school community.

WILL TEACHERS BECOME OBSOLETE?
August 7, 2019

One year after I wrote this blog post, most schools were not reopening for students due to the rise in the number of COVID-19 cases. I read that many schools would be adopting online programs as part of their distance learning curriculum. I was concerned. While I understood that students could fall further behind if they did not have access to appropriate grade level curriculum, I felt that these online programs had been hastily adopted without teacher training or buy-in and minimal evidence of their effectiveness.

Schools need to think about these questions if they choose to purchase a program for virtual learning. Will there be a positive and trusting relationship between the teacher and students? Will students feel comfortable asking questions if they don't understand? How do students reflect on their progress, and how does the teacher provide feedback to keep students moving forward in their learning goals? How does the teacher supplement these lessons to individualize the learning experiences for students? Does the teacher allow students choice in activities to keep them engaged in their own learning? Are there other options for students to learn the content besides the online program? Is the teacher allowed to deviate from the program and make decisions regarding what is best for students?

Build Teacher Capacity

I wanted a title for this blog that would make educators take notice. Technology is taking over many aspects of our society; we cannot let technology replace caring teachers in the classroom.

I happen to think that teaching is society's most important profession. The future of our kids is in the hands of educators who care and who are continuously learning and trying new strategies to engage and empower their students to be their best. The caring relationships that teachers create with their students can have a long-lasting, positive impact. Teaching is hard and requires stamina and the willingness to keep pushing forward even when things get challenging. It is not a job for the faint-hearted.

I believe that our society has diminished the important role of teachers. Political leaders claim that education is a priority, but funding is inadequate to update facilities, and schools must sometimes choose between classroom teachers and a librarian or an art or music or physical education teacher because there is not enough funding to go around. Many teachers are forced to get second jobs in order to pay their bills, young people are discouraged from becoming educators, and the public is quick to criticize schools for new ways of teaching and learning that they don't understand or that conflict with how they learned the same concept years ago when they were in school. It is no wonder that we have a teacher shortage; and it can only get worse.

As schools deal with a shortage of teachers and the availability of technology, what will they do? One option is to purchase a personalized learning program where students work at their level until they achieve mastery on the specific standard. Teachers review the data and then plan small group instruction for groups of students with similar areas of need. It sounds like a good plan, but does it work for every child? According to reports, the results are mixed. Some students would probably thrive in such a system because they are capable and competitive, but I think lots of kids would have difficulty. They would find it boring and would not be motivated to do their best. I also am concerned about whether learning for mastery in a personalized learning program translates to application of skills in real-life situations. Yet, I can see schools spending their funds on these types of programs as a solution to a shortage of teachers.

I am as guilty as the next person of using the self-checkout line at Walmart or going to the ATM machine to deposit or withdraw money instead of going to a sales clerk or a teller. We hear about robots replacing maids at hotels and robots efficiently preparing items for packaging and mailing at Amazon. Will this happen in our schools as well? Will teachers become obsolete? I certainly hope not.

That is why I think it's so important for teachers to tell their stories. They need to share with their students about why they chose to become teachers. Students need to hear from teachers about how much they love their job and how the little successes are sometimes the most gratifying. We need students to share their stories as well about teachers who believed in them and helped them overcome difficulties they were facing. Those are the memories our students will have when they move on from our classroom. It is what sustains them during challenges in their lives. They hear their teachers' voices: "I know you can do it. I care about you. I love how you never give up. I believe in you. Tell me what matters to you."

As an educator for 45 years, I cannot think of a more honorable or fulfilling profession than teaching. Educators and students, let's share that message with the public!

Let's Listen to Teacher Voices
December 9, 2020

When I became a principal back in 2003, I knew that our teachers were essential to moving our school forward, so I was puzzled by a question I was asked multiple times: How will you make decisions? I answered honestly that it depended. Sometimes I would have no choice in decisions; they might be state or district mandates. Other times I would seek feedback and we would have a discussion before we agreed on a course of action. Finally, there would be times when I would trust teachers to make their own decisions, and I would support them. In the months that followed, our teachers saw many examples of my decision-making process. I believe that being a good listener was essential, and I worked to build trusting relationships with our staff.

During the COVID-19 pandemic, I spoke with administrators and teachers who were struggling. This is a time when educators needed to support each other. If schools are going to get through this challenge and come out stronger and more confident, honest conversation between administrators and teachers is essential.

Recently, some teachers shared on Twitter that they are still reluctant and uncomfortable about speaking up in meetings for fear of being called a troublemaker. Those words surprised and saddened me because these are teacher leaders who are respected and publicly acknowledged for their voices and their views. I could understand how they felt, though.

I know that as a teacher, I was not someone who spoke up in faculty meetings. If I had a question or a comment, I contemplated whether I should raise my hand. Often, as I looked around, I saw faces that told me the teachers were anxious to be out of there; they had other things to do, and if I asked a question or made a comment, it might mean another 10 minutes or so before the meeting ended. So more often than not, I stayed silent.

I realized, though, that if I had a question, my colleagues might have a similar question. Yet we were reluctant to speak up. We encourage our students to speak up if they have questions or concerns, but as teachers, we are often hesitant to do so ourselves. We are more likely to be honest in smaller venues, or as is often the case, in the parking lot after the meeting is over.

When I became a principal, I knew that I wanted teachers to feel comfortable about asking questions or sharing their thoughts. Here are some strategies I used to get them to feel comfortable:

- Build relationships first; know your teachers so you can have casual conversations with them. They will feel more comfortable telling you what they really think of an idea or a proposal if they know you will understand their point of view. Our teachers knew that there were decisions we could not change, but sometimes, their concerns helped us make revisions that would make implementation smoother.
- Give teachers opportunities to meet and work with others who are not in their department or grade level. This is especially important with large faculties. We tried to start our meetings with an icebreaker or team-building activity where teachers were able to talk story or work with someone they normally didn't interact with. Starting out a meeting with a fun activity put people in a better mood after a sometimes hectic day.
- We gave our staff an opportunity to share their viewpoints in small groups. We often started by having them discuss the same or similar questions before reconvening in the large group. There are many different ways to share ideas that are generated; we don't have to take up time to have each group share out. Perhaps a spokesperson can share one big idea or concern they had. We could have groups write down ideas or responses to questions on Post-its that are then sorted into similar ideas. We could collect the group notes, summarize, and share with everyone. Or we could use a shared Google document where everyone had access and recorded their ideas. We can hear from more voices via small groups.
- Often when we go to workshops, meetings, or conferences, we are asked for feedback, but how honest are we? Do we add comments so the presenters could reflect on how they might improve their presentation? Or are we just checking off ratings that really don't provide much information about how the audience truly felt? Whenever I asked

teachers for feedback, I added a space for them to write their name and I asked open-ended questions. This was an opportunity for them to share any concerns or questions they had. If I wanted more feedback about their comment, they knew that I could have a conversation with them. The result was that our teachers were honest with their responses. I think they realized that we truly wanted to hear from them, and we took those questions and opinions into consideration when a final decision was made.

As a principal, I wanted our staff to feel comfortable when discussing issues, especially those that could be controversial. I remember when we proposed going for accreditation at a time when it was not required for elementary schools in Hawaiʻi. We knew it would take a lot of time and commitment, but after much sometimes heated discussion, we decided to go for it. Everyone was proud when we received a six-year accreditation term. This would not have been possible without everyone's buy-in and active participation, and even those who had been reluctant at first were visibly proud that they contributed to the process.

Much has been written recently about listening to student voices. We need to make time to listen to teacher voices as well.

BUILD TEACHER CAPACITY
Reflective Questions

- Are teachers at your school encouraged and recognized for what they can offer to their students and their colleagues? How?
- As a new teacher, what kind of support did you receive? As an experienced teacher, how do you support new teachers?
- What kind of support from your administrators is most valuable to you as a teacher?

- What kinds of opportunities do you have to give feedback to your administrator?
- How do you, as an educator, keep your personal learning relevant?
- If you could design a personalized professional development plan for yourself, what would it look like?
- What opportunities do you have to share your successes and challenges with your colleagues?
- Why is it important for educators to share their stories with their students? With their community? With the public?
- According to Kobe Bryant, "The most important thing is to try and inspire people so that they can be great in whatever they want to do." How are teachers at your school inspired so they can continue to do great things for their school, their students, and their community? ♥

NOTES

CHAPTER FIVE

PARTNERING WITH FAMILIES AND THE COMMUNITY

*"The greatness of a community
is most accurately measured by the
compassionate actions of its members."*
—*Coretta Scott King*

The home/school connection is an important factor in a student's success. In many communities, especially those in low socioeconomic areas, a home/school connection may be lacking. Single-parent families, parents working more than one job to make ends meet, and older children taking care of their younger siblings can be barriers to a positive home/school partnership and, ultimately, to student success. We were fortunate that parents at our school were involved in their children's education. We had great turnouts for school-wide events, and attendance at our student-parent-teacher conferences was high, with nearly 95% participation. Our Parent Community Networking Center (PCNC) coordinator actively sought opportunities for parents to volunteer at school activities and events.

Our school had an active partnership with a military unit. Members helped with activities such as campus beautification or hearing/vision screening. Others volunteered to read to classes on Dr. Seuss's birthday, or they helped set up and man a station during one of our many family events. There were many ways for community members to volunteer in our school.

Unfortunately, though, schools don't always share the great things they are doing, so the community may not be aware. The late US representative Mark Takai once asked me pointedly, "Why aren't schools sharing the great things they're doing with the community?" I realized that he was right, and we started writing articles about school activities for the local newspapers. Teachers wrote about special projects their students were doing, and we used social media to share about what was happening in classrooms and in our school. These little changes had positive impacts, and this led to a trusting relationship where parents and our school community felt comfortable about sharing concerns, questions, and suggestions. We also used social media as a means of communicating with our parents.

I was fortunate to have had the opportunity to lead a military-impacted school. Our staff was committed to doing their best despite the challenges associated with a transient community. It takes a special person to work at a school like ours, knowing that there will be a high rate of transience with students and families coming and going throughout the year. We saw students make huge progress during their time with us, and much of the credit goes to our committed staff, who often went above and beyond to work as a team with the students and their families to ensure progress. This relationship was especially critical when many of our families were experiencing deployment challenges.

I have been able to keep updated with many of our former families via social media. It makes me proud to see how well our former students have done socially, academically, athletically, in the creative arts, in leadership, or in community service when they've moved to new schools. That was always my hope, that our students be "ambassadors of aloha" when they transitioned to a new school.

I often dreamed about making our school a hub, the center of our community. What would that look like? Maybe we could have an adjoining pediatric clinic where parents could bring their children for immunizations or school physical exams. Perhaps there could be a drop-in child care clinic so parents can volunteer in classrooms or attend parent training or workshops. Maybe we could have a partnership with a university and offer college classes in the evenings when classrooms are not being used. Unfortunately, this was just a pipe dream for me, but maybe other schools will be able to see this dream come to fruition.

In this chapter, I share how communication and engagement with our parents and the community were integral to the success of our school. Their combined experiences in our schools can make them our most effective advocates.

COMMUNICATING WITH OUR PARENTS
August 27, 2012

When I got my first teaching job with Head Start, there was no technology; we didn't even have a phone in our classroom. At the time, we were expected to make at least two home visits to each family during the school year, to involve parents as volunteers in the classroom, and to teach parenting skills. As a young teacher, I gained experience and confidence on how to engage parents as partners with the school, recognizing that parents are the first and most important teachers for their children. That home/school connection was essential as we worked together to prepare our students to be ready for kindergarten and beyond.

Today, we have many more ways to communicate with our families. A robust school and classroom website or blog is one way to share information, but newsletters, emails, phone calls, postings on social media, coffee hours, and parent/child activities are also effective. At our school, we also asked for feedback each year via a School Community Council survey, and the results as well as the comments provided us with information about how parents felt about teaching and learning at our school as well as other areas for improvement.

When I wrote this blog post back in August 2012, I realized that we were making strides in keeping our families informed as well as inviting them to be active partners in their child's education. Like anything else, however, there was always room for improvement.

The pandemic showed us that the home/school connection is so important. Parents learned how to support their children in their classwork, and clear communication from the teacher was essential. Hopefully, teachers and parents realize that by working together, students will continue to progress.

I started off my career in education as a preschool Head Start teacher, and I strongly believe in the power of partnerships with parents. Head Start, which is a program for disadvantaged preschoolers, emphasizes that parents are their child's first teachers. I saw firsthand the many positive benefits of involving parents in the classroom or at school. As a young teacher, I realized that we should be creating those opportunities to invite parent volunteers into our classroom to work with students, not just to do clerical types of tasks. Involving parents as volunteers in the classroom effectively raised the adult-to-student ratio and had the added benefit of building capacity in the parents to learn skills and strategies for working with their own children at home.

Many university education programs do not teach courses on how to work with or communicate with parents, and, therefore, teachers do not always see the benefits of building that partnership. New teachers are often overwhelmed with the responsibilities of learning the culture of the school, planning standards-based lessons in the different curricular areas, and dealing with classroom management. They often do not realize the benefits of building strong parent partnerships even before school begins, which can start with something as simple as a welcome letter. A telephone call or a short note or email/text message to share something positive can work wonders, too. When a positive relationship between home and school is fostered, the child is the ultimate beneficiary.

Last year, our school decided to invest in an education website service that we hoped would help us communicate more effectively with parents and the school community. Our school website serves as an information system for site visitors and acts as an intermediary between the numerous stakeholders in the educational process.

Although we continuously updated the website last school year, survey results indicated that 60% of our parents never logged on to get information about our school. We realized that if we are to improve the percentage of parents accessing our website, we needed to give them a reason to get on, and after discussions, we decided to encourage teachers to create class web pages. To get to the class web page, parents would have to access the school site first.

Some teachers had been using class web pages as a way to communicate with parents about upcoming activities or homework assignments, to share information about the curriculum or to post classroom photos. We noticed that there were fewer parent complaints from those classes with web pages. So this year, we "highly encouraged" teachers to create class web pages or blogs. Right now, about 90% of the teachers have class web pages, although several are still "under construction." For the most part, I am impressed with the quality; they are creative, attractive, and contain lots of valuable information for parents. We're hoping that the up-front investment will lead to positive relationships and better communication with our parents.

It wasn't easy, and for many of our teachers, we were asking them to do something that was not in their comfort zone. However, we are fortunate to have teachers who volunteered to help their colleagues get their web pages set up. Once they got started, some teachers took off, and I am amazed at the individualization of each web page. We're sending out the parent activation codes this week, and I am hopeful that this year, our survey results will show an increase in the number of parents who are accessing our school website as a vehicle to get information.

Engaging Our School Community through Social Media
February 27, 2013

I knew that social media could be a powerful tool to communicate with our families. At first, I used Twitter and invited families to follow me. I shared announcements or upcoming events, but it was primarily one-way communication, and I didn't know how many families were actually reading my tweets. I knew there had to be a better platform, and that's when we started our Facebook page. I was familiar with Facebook, which made posting photos and information easier, and I noticed that parents were signing up in larger numbers than when we were using Twitter.

I started carrying my phone with me throughout the day, taking photos and sharing them on Facebook. Parents appreciated seeing what was going on in classrooms, and they were excited to share with their followers when their child appeared in a photo. Facebook opened up communication with our families and school community.

In February 2013, our School Community Council decided to host our semiannual School Community Meeting via a Facebook event. It was such a success, and even parents who were off-island at that time were able to join in and participate. It was a great way to get feedback from our families!

Ninety-nine percent of our students are from military-impacted families, and transitions and deployments are challenges we face as we seek to engage them as integral members of our school community. Our parents are supportive of the school, and school-wide events such as our recent student-led conferences, musical performances, and book fairs are well attended. However, results from our annual School Community Council survey indicated that communication was a major concern of parents, so we made a concerted effort to improve home/school communication.

We started by changing our school website. Initially, it was a lot of work and planning, but today, we pride ourselves on our website, which includes lots of information and resources for parents to access as well as updates about upcoming school events. New parents often share that they requested housing in our geographical area after finding out they were coming to Hawai'i and checking out our school web page. Additionally, most of our teachers created a class web page, and this also helped to bridge the gap between home and school.

Because social media is such an important part of our parents' lives, we decided to use Facebook as a means of communication. Our Hale Kula Eagles Facebook group has grown to several hundred members, and upcoming events are shared and photos are posted to keep members updated. Facebook allows families who have left us to find out what's happening at our school, and in turn, we can find out how our former students are doing at their new school. Facebook has been a wonderful way to keep in touch! We also publish Hale Kula Highlights at least once weekly, and the blog is sent directly to the email of those who've subscribed. Parents and staff share that they appreciate these weekly reminders of upcoming events and activities.

Our School Community Council is required to hold School Community Meetings at least twice per year to get feedback regarding our Academic Plan. This has been a major challenge for us. In the past, we held meetings in the mornings, or just before school ended for the day, or in the evening, and each time, very few parents attended or participated in the discussions. We even paired these meetings with a student performance, but parents weren't interested in giving feedback to us on how to improve teaching and learning at Hale Kula. After all, they were there to watch/videotape their children's performance.

After much discussion, we decided to try something different this year. We decided to host a virtual School Community Meeting using Facebook as the venue. Since parents were familiar with the US Army Garrison Hawaii Facebook Town Hall meetings, we thought we might get better participation than if we held a meeting at school. Here's the invitation that was posted:

> When: Monday, February 25, 2013
>
> Time: 6:00 p.m. until 7:00 p.m.
>
> Description: We are hosting a virtual School Community Meeting (following the format of the USAG Town Hall meeting). The purpose is to get input and suggestions on how we can craft our Academic Plan for SY2013–2014 to best reflect the needs of our school while following the Department of Education's Strategic Plan and the district mandates.
>
> Any posts or comments should be respectful. We will remove any comments or questions that are perceived as inappropriate or disrespectful.
>
> We will respond to all questions, but depending on the number of questions/comments we receive, we will prioritize our responses according to those with the greatest impact on our school community.
>
> Thank you for joining this event!

Frankly, we did not know what to expect, but a virtual meeting would allow anyone to join from their computer or mobile device wherever they happened to be at the time. We agreed to ask questions to get feedback rather than having parents post random comments or concerns. Our focus would be on getting input from parents on issues such as attendance, improving achievement in reading and math, keeping our students safe at school, and improving parent engagement and communication.

I am still amazed at the number of comments and posts we received during our virtual School Community Meeting! The participation was nonstop with nearly 200 responses, suggestions, comments, and lots of great ideas in just over one hour! Our challenge now is to take those ideas and to see how we might be able to implement them to improve student achievement as well as to address issues of traffic, safety, communication, and student well-being.

Think about it. Would we be able to get that kind of feedback if we held a face-to-face meeting? Absolutely not! People who might have been reluctant to speak up in a public meeting were able to share concerns or ask questions in a virtual venue. We could hear from anyone who had something to contribute, and everyone was respectful with their comments. We cannot guarantee that everyone's suggestions will be implemented, but we will at least consider them.

Everyone's time is so valuable, and finding ways to accommodate the needs of our families is important. I am so grateful that our School Community Council took this leap and decided to host a virtual meeting. Perhaps other schools will be willing to give it a try!

The Challenges and Rewards of Leading a Military-Impacted School
April 21, 2013

This blog post was written in April 2013 when we celebrated the Month of the Military Child, and I wanted to share how proud I was to be the principal of Hale Kula Elementary School. When I became principal in 2003, I stated that my goal was to give students a unique cultural experience they would remember for the rest of their lives. I wanted our students to remember that they had attended school in Hawaiʻi, and I wanted them to take with them the values and experiences that they can only get here in this special place.

I never thought that I would remain at one school for over fifteen years, but being the principal at our school made me more appreciative of what our military-impacted families sacrifice for our country. It was my honor to be the principal of our school.

I attended a high school where about 25% of the students were military dependents. When I started teaching, about half of my years were spent on a military base, working with students from military families. However, I never realized the full impact of the challenges these families face, as well as their resiliency to deal with these challenges, until I became the principal of a military-impacted school.

I have been the principal of Hale Kula for over ten years. Back in February 2003 when I was first appointed, we had a student population of about 450 students. Today, we more than doubled that number with our student enrollment fluctuating between 950 and 1,050 students this school year. The change in the number of students has much to do with the privatization of housing on military bases and the high occupancy rate because of these beautiful new homes. As the principal of a school with 99% military dependents, the way we do things, our culture, is different from that of a "local" school.

I recently read an article in an issue of *Principal* magazine titled "Helping Military Children Feel 'At Ease.'"[12] Few people realize that the military is a culture, and students face unique challenges as a result of being a military dependent. Moving to Hawai'i can be exciting, but it can add to the stresses that families face. Being so far from family and other systems of support is not easy.

Transitions are a major challenge for some military-impacted students. Our students might attend three different schools in one year, and possibly many more before graduating from high school. Because the Schofield Inn is within our school's geographical boundaries, we have a high number of transitions each school year. Students are enrolled when they are at the Schofield Inn, but unfortunately, once a family is assigned permanent housing, the student may have to leave our school if they will not be living in our area. Imagine having to be the "new kid in the class" several times in a school year. It takes a student with confidence and resiliency to be able to make the adjustment each time he/she is enrolled in a new school.

Oftentimes, the curriculum and the school rules and procedures are different, and when a child moves in the middle of the year, adjusting can be a challenge. We have had students enroll after being out of school for several months because they were visiting family on the way to Hawaiʻi. As a result, military students can have gaps in their learning and may have missed important instruction that can impact their learning. Unless the teacher is cognizant of these gaps, the student may go through the rest of the year without learning something that is an important foundational skill not just for that school year, but in future years as well.

When I became the principal ten years ago, our families did not have to worry about deployments. Then things changed in the Middle East. The first deployment took place nearly nine years ago, and after that, a significant percentage of our students were experiencing the challenges of dealing with a parent who was away from the family, in harm's way. Some families faced multiple deployments while they were attending our school. The challenges of deployment didn't necessarily end when a parent returned home. Families had to readjust to having a parent back home, and sometimes, the parent changed after experiencing trauma during the deployment. Some students and families deal with deployment challenges positively while others have great difficulty.

These challenges in military schools need to be addressed, and because we have flexibility over how we spend the funds allocated to us, we have been able to create positions at Hale Kula to address some of these issues. For example, we have four counselors as well as a school-based behavioral health therapist. They provide essential support for students who may be experiencing difficulties that are impacting their success in school. Our Transition Center coordinator greets all new families to share information about our school and our policies prior to the child's first day. Additionally, the transition coordinator checks on new students to ensure that he/she is adjusting to their new school. Our Primary School Adjustment Project child associate works with younger students who may be experiencing problems with adjustment caused by deployment or a new school. We are also fortunate to have the support of the US Army Garrison Hawaii through their School Liaison Officers as well as a partnership with Tripler Army Medical Center, which provides support through their School Mental Health Team. Our school staff works closely with district support personnel as well as the Tripler team to ensure that programs and supports are in place to ensure the success of all students and their families.

The "'At Ease'" article shared suggestions for schools that can have a positive impact on military students and their families. Perhaps the most important support, however, comes from the teacher in the classroom. Our teachers are a special group; they deal with transitioning students (sometimes several a week); they provide interventions for students who may enter their classroom with significant learning gaps, and they deal with deployment challenges that may affect a student's behavior and academics in the classroom. Parents have shared that they appreciate the support from their child's teacher or from another adult in the school.

It is equally important, though, to address the needs of the families. As a school, we made it a priority to plan activities for families so they can connect with other families—activities such as after-school parent/child workshops, book fair family events, parenting trainings, or student performances. Additionally, we have been communicating with parents through social media as well as a weekly blog and our school website. Parents appreciate being updated about what's going on in school and being able to communicate with the school via technology, especially when there is only one adult at home.

I am proud of our school and the supports and services we provide for our military students and their families. Our goal is to ensure the success of every student and to provide them with the tools to be independent and to be responsible for their own learning and individual growth. This means that we need to be aware of the military culture and addressing the challenges of our students and their families.

Partnering with Families and the Community 137

Giving Thanks, 2017
November 21, 2017

I first wrote a blog post for Thanksgiving in 2012, and in subsequent year, I updated and shared my appreciation to the school community. This one, written in 2017, was my last Thanksgiving post as a principal. I am grateful that I was able to share my appreciation with the school community on Thanksgiving Day. Every year, I added the following introduction to an updated post:

> *When I first started blogging, this was one of my first posts. That was back in 2012, and since then, I have continued to blog and share my thoughts with our school community. I think this "old" post is still reflective of how I feel about our school, so I am reposting and updating it since so many of our families are new to our school. Happy Thanksgiving to our DKIES ʻohana!*

This Thanksgiving Day in 2017 is a perfect opportunity to reflect on my principalship at Daniel K. Inouye Elementary School and all that I am thankful for. What makes a school special and unique is its people, and DKIES is no exception.

All of my schooling has been here in Hawaiʻi, and I can't imagine being uprooted in the middle of the year and having to go to a new school, make new friends, learn new rules, procedures, and curriculum, and adjust to these new surroundings. Yet our DKIES students are asked to do this not once but multiple times in their school careers. More often than not, this is occurring while a parent is attending training or is deployed. Our students make the best of their situation even while they are missing a parent who may be off-island for training exercises or who may be deployed and in harm's way. I marvel at their resilience, and my hope is that they will take what they've learned at DKIES about aloha and share it with others when they leave Hawaiʻi. At DKIES, Eagles Pride means to: "Take care of yourself. Take care of others. Take care of our school." This is a message we hope they will live throughout their education years.

I am grateful to the DKIES parents who support our school and trust us with their children. Military parents' lives are so different from what I experienced as a young mom when I had family and friends to support me. Being uprooted from their system of support is a challenge, and their confidence in our school to take care of their children is a responsibility we take seriously. To the soldier parents who have committed to serving and protecting our nation, I send my heartfelt thanks. And to the spouse who is left behind to take care of the home and the family while the soldier is absent, you deserve kudos for all you do. It takes a strong person to accept and adapt to military life, and often, you turn every new change of duty station into an adventure and a learning opportunity for your family. Mahalo for all you do.

I am so honored to be at a school with such a great staff. I love going to work every day because I work with people who care about our school as much as I do. Others may not realize the challenges of working with a highly transient military population, but your commitment and pride in your work is what makes our school so special. I hope you realize the positive impact you have, long after the students and families have left DKIES and Hawai'i. I am truly proud to be part of our DKIES 'ohana.

Four and a half years ago, we were one of the original schools on military bases in the United States to receive funding to upgrade and renovate our facilities. In 2016, all of the construction was completed, and our school was renamed after a great American hero from Hawai'i, Daniel K. Inouye. When I first became principal of Hale Kula Elementary School in February 2003, I would never have imagined how the school would transform during my tenure. I am so appreciative to Congress and the State of Hawai'i Legislature for funding our $33.2 million project, to everyone who made this project possible, and to our school community for their patience and support throughout the challenging construction phases. It is humbling to realize all that went into this project to benefit our students now and in the future.

I am truly blessed with a wonderful and loving family, supportive friends, a job that I love, good health, living in a place that many consider paradise. I couldn't ask for more.

POSITIVE RELATIONSHIPS WITH PARENTS OF OUR STUDENTS WITH SPECIAL NEEDS
February 16, 2018

Too often, parents come to Individualized Education Program (IEP) meetings only because they have to be there, not because they want to. They don't feel they have anything to contribute when in reality, they know more about their child than anyone else at the table. Putting parents at ease and ensuring that they share their concerns and suggestions were integral to the creation of their child's IEP.

Not everything went smoothly; sometimes, it took several meetings before we could finalize a plan for the student. There were times when an advocate was present, which could negatively impact the relationship between the family and the school team. But there were many, many more successes.

This was an important blog post for me to write shortly before I retired in 2018. As an administrator sitting in on IEP meetings, I knew that I had a crucial role in ensuring that our students with special needs received the support and services they needed to be successful.

I sit in on a lot of IEP meetings as an administrator. There have been a few that were challenging, but overall, our school welcomes the opportunity to work with parents to create an Individualized Education Program that meets the needs of the special needs student. I feel that we are doing well at our school because we have great staff who truly provide quality learning experiences for our students. Our staff cares for our special needs students, and that is reflected in our classrooms as well as in our positive relationships with the child and his/her family.

The purpose of this blog post is to remind ourselves that parents are the most important person at an IEP meeting. They know their child best, and it behooves us to listen and learn from them. Sometimes parents are uncomfortable at the meeting and may be reluctant to say much, thinking that the school knows best. They may even feel a bit guilty that somehow they have failed in their role as parents. As the school team, we try to put parents at ease by having them share about their child. Tell us what your child is like at home. What does he/she like to do? What are your goals for your child? This information is so important because it helps the team to build a stronger relationship with the child as well as the parents. We encourage teachers to get to know their students because doing so can truly make a difference for that child. It is no different for special needs students; in fact, it can be even more important for that child to have a teacher who knows what he/she likes or what is frustrating or what might be motivating. There have been meetings where parents clearly felt emotional when asked to share about their child. It can be difficult to share the challenges they face at home every day. Those insights can help us, the child's IEP team. We can find out so much about a child by asking his/her parents for their input, and the IEP we create together will be a stronger document as a result.

I wish that all teachers would be required to spend time in a special needs class before having their own classroom. It gives a whole new perspective on what it means to work as a team to help a student continue to grow and be successful. The one year I taught a class of special education preschoolers gave me the insight and empathy I need to be a successful administrator sitting in on IEP meetings. To this day, I remember those students and what they taught me, like Joshua who spoke gibberish when he started. His mom shared that every week, they called her parents on the mainland, and usually, he wouldn't want to talk to them, or if he did, his grandparents had no idea what he was saying. Towards the end of the year, Joshua's mom shared that her parents were crying when she finally got the phone away from him the previous evening. His grandparents could understand what Joshua was so excited to share with them. I remember Sam, who didn't walk when he started but was so determined to do so. At Preschool Play Day, where all the district's special needs PK students gathered for fun and games with lots of soldier volunteers, the last activity was to run from one side of the gym to the other. Sam started with his walker. The other kids ran and celebrated when they got to the other side. Sam kept going. He was the only one on the gym floor, and everyone was on the sidelines, cheering him on. He would stop to rest, then continue. The roar was deafening when he crossed that line, and a soldier picked him up and carried him to the loud cheers of the whole gym. I still get tears in my eyes when I remember that moment, and it was 30 years ago.

The point I'm trying to make is this. To us, that child is a student, and we do our best to help him/her to be successful in school. To his/her parents, that special needs child is their world, and they want him/her to be successful in life. I will admit that when I became an administrator, receiving training on the nuts and bolts of special education and IEPs, I was told to "be tough" and "know the law" and "don't give in." I didn't receive any training on how to work with parents, and yet, that is what makes or breaks a relationship. Each one of those special needs students and their families that I have had the privilege to work with taught me that "it takes a village" to educate a child, and the home/school relationship is crucial to a child's success.

PARTNERING WITH THE COMMUNITY
March 3, 2021

Partnering with the community was essential to our school's success. As I was finalizing this book, I realized that I had not blogged specifi-

cally about this, even though community involvement was essential to our school.

Because we are a public school located on a military base, it was natural that much of our support came from the military community. However, our school also received support from the greater community via organizations such as the Lions and Kiwanis, Leilehua High School student clubs, and the Kokua Foundation, and through grants and support from many other organizations.

I reviewed my blog and pulled relevant information from different places to write this section. Partnering with the community was essential to the success of our school and provided important learning opportunities and activities for our students and our staff.

They say, "It takes a village to raise a child," and this is true of schools. It is the partnership and the involvement of many different organizations and volunteers that made a difference at our school.

The support from US Army leadership was essential. A school liaison officer (SLO) served as a bridge for communication between the school and the military. The SLO was trained in mediation, and when concerns were raised by parents or the school, the SLO was able to bring the parties together to resolve the issue. Military and school leaders met quarterly and exchanged important information so we could do our best for our students and their families. We also shared challenges we were facing, and the military leaders were helpful in providing assistance and support. In addition, the Joint Venture Education Forum (JVEF) was a partnership between all branches of the military, military-impacted schools, and the business community. JVEF meetings were an opportunity to share concerns and to be a part of the solution to improve the educational experiences for our military students.

We were fortunate to have a partnership with Tripler Army Medical Center (TAMC). The doctors and social workers were integral members of our School Mental Health Team. When we were meeting to discuss plans for our new school buildings, we made sure that there would be separate rooms for the Tripler doctors and social workers so they could meet with our students and parents in a setting that met medical privacy guidelines. For parents and teachers, having the Tripler staff on our campus was more than a convenience. It was an important partnership, working as a team with students and their families who were experiencing mental health challenges. Our partnership with TAMC was a successful model that could and should be explored at other schools.

We had an active partnership with an Army unit, HHBN 25th ID, and we could count on them to provide volunteers whenever we had an event or an activity at our school. These partnerships were an opportunity for young soldiers to get involved in the community and to hone leadership skills. Volunteers helped with our complex cross country event, came to read to our students, helped out with campus beautification, and enjoyed constructing a maze for the Cardboard Challenge. Whenever we needed volunteers to set up for a special event or to lead an activity, they were there. We were very grateful for their assistance, support, and commitment to our school.

We invited community speakers to our school, and they shared about climate change, the homeless, endangered plants and animals, fire safety, coding, energy efficiency, and other important topics. Authors came to share their books and shared about the writing process. Students were able to interact with musicians and artists, and architects shared the process for designing new buildings. We actively interacted with the community, which brought real-world relevance to what students were learning.

Our school hosted many family events with volunteers from the community. One example was Super STEM Saturday for Girls, an event which involved many volunteers from the community, including our local high school, the complex area team, the University of Hawai'i, and numerous engineering organizations, among them those from the Army. Our keynote speaker for the event was one of my former students. Jennifer Eugenio is now an engineer with the Army Corps of Engineers, and I was excited when she said she would be part of our inaugural event. Jennifer is young, smart, articulate, and a wonderful role model for our girls. She gave good advice to our young engineers: Keep up your good grades. Get used to working in teams. Explore and try new things. Question everything. Never be afraid to make mistakes. Great advice for our girls and their parents! One of the great things about our Super STEM Saturday event was that our girls had the opportunity to work with lots of female engineers and scientists. They were wonderful role models for our girls, helping them realize that STEM can be fun and challenging.

The community is an essential component of any school. In a best-case scenario, the school can and should be the hub, the central focus of a community with members advocating and providing support. Additionally, by involving community members in the school, our students may realize the real-world relevance of what they are learning.

Partnering with Families and the Community
Reflective Questions

- Give examples of what "partnering with families and the community" means to you.
- What kind of training on working with parents and the community did you receive in your university coursework? Would this have made a difference in how you view parents and the community as partners? How?
- How do you communicate with parents and/or the community so they are aware of what you are doing in your classroom or your school? Why is communication important?
- How do you use social media to effectively communicate with parents and the community? How has this helped you in your role as an educator?
- The pandemic has negatively impacted funding for education. Besides financial support, what kinds of support

can parents and the community provide to enhance education for your students?
- According to Coretta Scott King, "The greatness of a community is most accurately measured by the compassionate actions of its members." How do the actions of your school community positively impact the larger community?" ♥

NOTES

CHAPTER SIX

WHAT DOES THE FUTURE HOLD FOR EDUCATION?

"Change before you have to."
—*Jack Welch*

What does the future hold for education, not just in Hawai'i, but in our nation? Although some things have changed, the basic structure of school hasn't changed much. Students still sit in classrooms, often in rows facing the teacher. Bells ring to indicate when it is time to transition to a different course or a different teacher. Students go through a progression of grade levels from kindergarten through grade 12 with suggested standards of what they should be learning. They are assessed on what was taught, and quarterly report cards as well as standardized tests inform parents about how well the student is doing in school. After 12 or 13 years, students graduate, receive a diploma, and decide what to do for the next few years. Usually, the options are to continue their education, to go to work, or to join the military.

We are in turbulent times; we need to refresh and regroup and regrow our community, our state, our nation, the world. What kind of world are we leaving for our children and future generations when we face problems such as climate change, a huge federal deficit, a polarized and divided populace, chronic disease, hunger, homelessness, and trash? We have created these problems, and now is the time for our schools to involve students in opportunities to discuss possible solutions.

During the pandemic, I saw many posts on social media from teachers in Hawai'i and in other parts of our world doing extraordinary things. They were learning as they were doing and providing their students with creative and engaging lessons, all while quarantined, learning how to use new tools to communicate with students and families. They were collaborating with other educators, problem-solving, asking questions of each other, and holding virtual conferences so they could share ideas. It was amazing, and this collaboration needs to continue even after this pandemic is over.

As a lifelong educator who remains passionate about improving education, I believe it takes the commitment of everyone to engage in a discussion to ensure that our children are prepared for their future through a quality public education system. This pandemic exposed problems that had been festering for years with no long-term solutions. It's not too late. We have been given a unique opportunity to make needed changes in how we move forward to address our education challenges. We all need to do our part to ensure that we can make positive changes for the sake of our children and future generations. It starts with each of us.

How Can We Improve Special Education Services in Hawai'i?
February 7, 2016

When I began teaching Head Start back in 1973, 10% of our students were required to be diagnosed with special needs. I recall that those students generally had speech delays, and they received speech therapy services. In 1975, Public Law 94-142 was passed, guaranteeing a "free and appropriate public education" (FAPE) for all children from three to 21 years of age. At Head Start, we were now required to meet with the child's team and write a plan to address the areas of need. That initial experience with special education was important in my development as a teacher and an administrator.

Teaching preschool special education at Wheeler Elementary was one of the best learning experiences for me. Those 12 students with a range of diagnoses, including speech and language delays, autism, developmental delays, and multiple disabilities, taught me so much. I learned that early interventions, working as a team, and addressing goals and objectives consistently are essential for students with special needs. That year prepared me well for when I became an administrator.

When I wrote this blog post in February 2016, I had served on a committee to make recommendations regarding the Department of Education budget. Realizing the funding allocation as well as a shortage of staffing for special education got me thinking of ways we might improve special education services in our state.

Our school's special education department is wonderful. They conduct themselves professionally, rarely complain about high caseloads, work collaboratively with the whole team including parents, and do their best to implement their students' Individualized Education Program. Hawai'i is considered an overseas assignment for military families, and Tripler Army Medical Center is able to provide the level of services that families of students who have special needs may require, so our military-impacted school has a higher-than-usual percentage of students with IEPs.

In our country, every student is entitled to a free and appropriate public education (equality). To level the playing field, some students require additional services or supports in order to be successful (equity). Presently, all public schools in Hawai'i receive funding based on a per pupil allocation (equality). Additional funds are allocated for disadvantaged, English language learners, and special education students because they require more services and resources (equity).

Based on my experiences at our school, I would like to share some suggestions regarding special education in our state. Some of these are systemic changes that will require honest conversations with all those concerned with improving special education services in our Hawai'i public schools. This would include teacher preparation programs.

- First, let's grow our own within the DOE. Let's provide professional training for educational assistants at no cost to them. Last year, the Department spent $38 million on contracted provider services, primarily for students with an autism diagnosis. We can decrease that amount if we have certified staff within our schools to work with the students who benefit from that type of specific instruction.
- Next, let's do a better job of recruiting educational assistants (EAs) and providing incentives for them to take courses related to their job. We give teachers the opportunity to move up a step when they take classes and complete the requirements. Let's do the same for our EAs.
- Third, let's restructure our teacher education programs and have prospective educators enroll from their freshman year rather than waiting until they are juniors to be accepted into the College of Education. Get them in classrooms from their first semester in the program so they have many more opportunities to gain valuable hands-on experiences.
- Fourth, I'd like to see every teacher education program require their students to take classes and to spend at least a semester in a special education classroom. With a focus on Response to Intervention and co-teaching classrooms, all teachers should know how to analyze data and how to provide specific targeted instruction for those students who may be struggling. Fewer students may require special education services if we can identify and intervene early on before the gap widens.
- Additionally, every elementary teacher should be trained in multisensory strategies because children learn in different ways. One way of teaching may not be effective for all

students. If students are not learning the way they are being taught, then we need to change the way we are teaching. When we teach using multisensory strategies, we provide students with different ways to get the information and to make connections that are essential for learning.
- Finally, schools struggle to provide appropriate services for students who require more intensive services. Perhaps it's time to establish centers in every complex area for students with autism or for students with emotional needs who are not successful in their present placement. The goal would always be to provide the intensive services the student needs initially and to work with the staff to gradually integrate the student back to their home school. Those schools can also be training centers for university students who have committed to working with more challenging students. Perhaps we should also consider paying these teachers more since they are in a hard-to-fill area.

I believe that if we can implement these changes to our system, we will improve our services not only to students who are eligible for special education, but for all students. In the process, we may realize savings that can then be used for all students in our public schools. Funding will be more equitable, but we will continue to ensure equity for those who are eligible for services.

All Schools Deserve to Be Upgraded
October 16, 2016

Hale Kula, built in 1959, was fortunate to receive funding from the Department of Defense and the State of Hawaiʻi to transform our school to support 21st-century teaching and learning. This whole project has made me realize how important buildings are to a school. Most of our schools in Hawaiʻi were built for a different era with the factory model that was prevalent in education at that time. We need to invest in upgrading our schools. Once our construction project was complete, I realized that our teachers were doing their best to give our students 21st-century learning experiences without the proper infrastructure.

One of my suggestions is a public-private partnership. Although this idea is somewhat controversial, I think we need to look at all possible sources of revenue when we discuss ways to upgrade our schools.

Tomorrow, we officially celebrate the completion of the final phase of our three-plus-year project to upgrade our school as well as the renaming of our school to Daniel K. Inouye Elementary School. As I reflect on our journey as the first school in Hawaiʻi to qualify for the DOD-OEA funding for schools on military bases across the country, I realize that we have a responsibility to share our journey, to celebrate our success, and to hopefully make it possible to create a system that allows public-private partnerships to upgrade our schools in Hawaiʻi.

After President Obama was first elected, military parents met with Secretary of Defense Gates to share their concerns over the poor condition of schools on base. A facilities assessment was undertaken on all schools located on military bases in the country, and after a rating scale based on "condition" and "capacity," our school was number nine on the list of 157 schools. That started a whirlwind process to apply for a DOD-OEA grant to receive funding (80% of the project cost) to address areas of need in the assessment. Senator Daniel K. Inouye was instrumental in passage of a congressional allocation of $250 million in what would be one of his last major measures passed as the Senate Appropriations Committee chairperson. Through a charrette process involving a design team and the Department of Education, as well as school staff and the military, we envisioned 21st-century buildings where students are able to collaborate and communicate with others not just within their classroom but globally as well, and where critical thinking and creating are emphasized.

On July 1, 2013, we held a groundbreaking ceremony, and a little more than three years later, our project is complete. Throughout the three-phase process, I updated our community via a blog.[13] We realized that many of our students and their families would not be at our school to follow our progress to upgrade our facilities. As each phase was completed, I would ask myself how we got so lucky to be able to rebuild and renovate our school.

As a school located on a military base, we were fortunate to be able to access federal funds to address concerns noted in the facilities assessment. Eighty percent of the cost was provided by the DOD-OEA grant, and 20% was funded via a state legislative appropriation to our Department. For $6.6 million in state funds, we now have an administrative building that is much larger than the old one that was built in 1959. Our 10-classroom building with flexible learning spaces is so much more conducive to learning than the portable classrooms we were using. Our library is spacious, and the available resources as well as the Exploratopia Makerspace will empower our students to explore, discover, create, and share. Counselors and our School Mental Health Team from Tripler Army Medical Center have their own rooms for privacy (previously, they all shared a room), and now, we can meet as a faculty in a meeting room rather than in the cafeteria. And our covered play court? I pinch myself every time I go there. Our physical education teachers and our students will make great use of this facility, and we now have a place for our whole school to gather for assemblies and events.

But shouldn't all schools—not just schools on military bases—be able to reinvent and upgrade their school facilities? So many of our schools need to be renovated or upgraded, and funding from the legislature is limited. We need to think of other ways to upgrade our schools, many of which are already 50-plus years old.

The Hawai'i Institute for Public Affairs examined the issue of public-private partnerships to build 21st-century schools for Hawai'i's students and shared their ideas in "Systematic Approach to Building 21st-Century Schools: Experiences in the Aloha State."[14] Although a bill was passed by the state legislature and signed by the governor in 2011, we have not yet seen the impact on our schools. In fact, communities and legislators have to "fight" to get their share of funding to upgrade or to build new schools in growing communities, and the cost continues to increase each year.

When I became principal of our school in February 2003, I never dreamed that we would ever be allocated funds to upgrade our facilities. Now that our project is completed, I hope that our positive experience will start the discussion on how to provide this kind of opportunity for other schools that were built for a different generation of students. All students deserve it.

"BE A HERO. BE A TEACHER."
September 22, 2017

Teaching is not easy, and some years are more challenging than others. Not all teacher candidates have the kinds of experiences or the strong mindset that are needed to be confident in the classroom when things get difficult. Some of our best teachers had rough starts with challenges they didn't anticipate, but they were resilient and did not give up.

I wrote this blog post in 2017 after reading a news article about a program funded by the legislature to recruit substitute teachers or educational assistants to enter a program to earn a teaching degree. Although I thought this was a great idea, I also believe that we must do a better job of preparing our teacher candidates so they remain in the profession.

It always saddens me when parents tell me that they discouraged their child from going into education. It was especially disheartening when the parent was an educator. We don't need teachers to be heroes, but we do need them to understand that the work they do is important to the future of our communities, our state, and our nation, and that it will not be easy.

Recently, the news media here in Hawai'i announced a program to train and retain teachers here in Hawai'i. I shared this article[15] on Facebook with this statement: "Being an educator is hard work but I have never regretted my decision. Even on the most challenging days, there is something positive to reflect on. What could be more important than positively impacting our young people so they are inspired to make a difference in our world?" I truly believe that teaching is an art, that great teachers help create excited learners who find their passion and pursue their dreams. I appreciate that the legislature allocated more funding for "our own" who aspire to become teachers, especially those who may already be in the schools and have demonstrated their commitment to education. I sincerely hope that these individuals will take advantage of this opportunity to achieve their dream of positively impacting our young people as a teacher.

The media campaign to "Be a Hero. Be a Teacher." is a great start, but it's going to take more than that to raise confidence in our school system and our educators. Negative comments from the public are the norm, not just in Hawai'i, but nationally as well. It behooves us all to participate in conversations about how our public school system can be improved, but we must be open to new ideas. Here are some suggestions to start that discussion:

- University programs should follow the lead of the University of Hawai'i–West O'ahu. Education majors begin taking courses and fieldwork in their freshman year. They are in classrooms and taking education courses from the beginning. The more experience these education majors have, the better prepared they will be when they have their own classrooms.
- All teachers—especially those in elementary schools—should be required to take classes in strategies to teach struggling learners. Students enter kindergarten with a wide range of experiences and challenges that impact their school readiness. Recognizing a student's deficits and providing early, consistent interventions using research-based strategies can mean the difference between catching up to peers or requiring more intensive services in a later grade.

- Our youngest learners in kindergarten should be "learning by doing." We weren't expected to know all the letters and sounds and numbers when we were in kindergarten. Yes, I know that was a long time ago and the world has changed since then, but let's face it—some students are not ready to read and write in kindergarten. They need more time to develop their vocabulary, to practice their fine motor skills, to listen and to contribute to a conversation, to explore and discover new information, and to create and share what they are learning. They should be looking at books and hearing stories read to them, learning to play cooperatively with others, practicing to share and to think about others' feelings and to problem-solve when things aren't going their way. They shouldn't have to sit and write letters and numbers that have no meaning for them—yet. Let's acknowledge that learning through play or learning by doing is more developmentally appropriate for our young learners.
- The world has changed drastically since I went to school, but schools basically have remained the same. We have charter schools that are implementing innovative practices, but the other public schools have changed very little, structure-wise. Schools are still separated by grade levels and grade level bands—elementary, middle, and high school. Schools still have schedules where students start and end at the same time. There are standards for each grade level, and despite starting school with different skill sets, all students are expected to be at a certain place at the end of the year. If we assume that we all learn at different rates and have different interests, we might want to rethink the structure of school to be more flexible where age is not the defining criteria and where students might work in multiage environments on collaborative projects that demonstrate their mastery of necessary skills.

- As an early childhood major, I strongly believe in early interventions and the power of parental involvement to make a difference for students. University coursework rarely includes strategies for working with parents, and teachers are often uncomfortable having parent volunteers in their classroom. Yet, parents can be our best advocates; they see how hard teachers work, how patient they are, and how challenging the job can be. Volunteers in the classroom can mean more eyes and more support for students. Parents are their child's first and most important teacher; let's value their input because they know their child best.

As an educator for over 40 years, I can say unequivocally that teaching is an honorable profession, and I can't think of any job that is more important for our society.

WILL WE HAVE THE COURAGE TO CHANGE?
April 12, 2020

I wrote this blog post in the early months of the pandemic when I thought we would be sheltering in place for only a few months. I believed that although students had lost their fourth quarter of school year 2019–2020, school would resume for the following school year. I recognized that our lives were changing as a result of COVID-19. This blog took a bit longer to write, but I felt it was important to ask ourselves to think about what we might change, not just in schools, but in all aspects of our lives.

Unfortunately, as I write this in 2021, the pandemic is still not over, and life has not gone back to normal. The impact has been devastating, with many businesses shutting down and unemployment at record levels. Furloughs and layoffs were being discussed as ways to balance the budget, and schools in Hawaiʻi were asked to submit a drastically reduced spending plan for next school year.

It is imperative that we have the courage to change what and how we do things. William Archer Ward stated, "The pessimist complains about the wind; the optimist expects it to change; the realist adjusts the sails." It's time to adjust our sails.

I've been thinking about what life will be like post-COVID-19. This has been a challenging time for all of us, and because we are social creatures of habit, making drastic changes in how we live day-to-day during this lockdown has been difficult.

For myself, part of the older generation that is most impacted by this virus, staying at home has now become a way of life. Although we are both retired, my husband and I continued to have a schedule with appointments, luncheons, the gym, meetings, and other activities that kept us busy. It's a bit strange to see, "No more events. Your day is clear," every day when I put my watch on in the morning. This stay-at-home order means planning what we need, so I go to the market once a week instead of every day or every other day like I often did pre-pandemic. It means going for walks twice a day if the weather is nice: once with my husband, Randy (who now appreciates walking), and once with our dog, Iwak. It means more handwashing and keeping sanitizing wipes in my purse. It means calling my 92-year-old mom to make sure she is okay and checking in more often with our son and grandsons who live on the mainland. It means physical distancing and wearing a mask when we go shopping to ensure others' safety as well as ours. It means keeping up with the latest news on COVID-19 but turning to a different TV station when the news gets too depressing. It means appreciating that we are doing okay and that we are weathering this silent storm.

But there are times when I think about what will happen when this is all over. Will we just go back to what we were doing before this pandemic disrupted our lives? Or will we use what we are learning now to make major changes?

My parents' generation lived through the Great Depression as well as World War II. I believe it is why they were resourceful throughout their lives. They saved for a rainy day, and they only spent what they could afford, choosing to go without rather than go into debt. Today's generation is different. Things are so accessible to us and we are wasteful, not just with what we purchase but with our time as well. COVID-19 has disrupted our daily lives and gives us a perfect opportunity to reflect and to change what we're doing to improve our quality of life. And it gives our systems a chance to reinvent themselves, too. A proverb states that, "Necessity is the mother of invention." If so, here are some of my thoughts for discussion:

Schools

Now that buildings are closed, probably for the rest of the school year, educators have had to reinvent how they provide learning opportunities for their students as well as professional development and collaborative opportunities for their staff. By using virtual tools such as videoconferencing, online classrooms, blogs, videos and tons of other resources that are and have been made available for their use, teachers are expanding their resource library to engage and empower students in their learning. School building closures have brought to light the reality about the important roles that education plays in our communities. Schools are not just places for learning; they also provide students with a sense of safety and continuity; it is where students may learn how to navigate important social-emotional and friendship issues; and schools address health and well-being challenges. The closing of schools has given educators an opportunity to try new ideas. I sincerely hope schools discuss how they can use what they have learned through this unprecedented time to change teaching and learning. Here are a few ideas that educators might consider: blended learning (face-to-face as well as collaborating via technology) for all students; passion projects or project-based learning based on student interests as well as current issues; working on projects across grade levels or with different schools across the state or nation; online classes or internships in the community for high school students, where they can work anywhere, anytime and be better prepared for their future; or employing different ways of assessing student learning such as video portfolios, performances, or presentations to a panel. Schools need to be relevant if we want students and educators to be engaged and empowered; this is a good time to implement new ideas.

Small Businesses

Small businesses have been hit hardest, I believe, during this time of sheltering in place, and having government funds for loans is essential. After all, small business owners are crucial partners in our communities. It is heartwarming to see that some businesses are reinventing themselves during this difficult time. For example, restaurants have expanded their takeout services or provide free delivery to customers; we are encouraged to order meals from them. Imagine if restaurants continue this service when they reopen; it is possible that more staff could be hired. This is a great time for businesses to be looking ahead to streamline their operations, to make their products more accessible to the public, to offer their products online, or to try something new to bring in customers once they are able to reopen. This can be a time to experiment with an idea on a smaller scale in order to get feedback. Businesses are at the heart of our communities, and now more than ever, they need our support.

Diversifying Our Economy

Hawaiʻi relies so heavily on our tourism industry. There were over 10.4 million visitors to our state in 2019. While that may be good for the economy, generating income for our state, we cannot rely on tourism to fill our state coffers, especially in these times when tourism has literally come to a halt. Tourism means additional cars on the road and spending extra time in our cars, stuck in traffic. Without tourists filling our hotel rooms, many workers lose their jobs. We cannot rely only on tourism. In the past, Hawaiʻi has tried to expand our innovation technology industry via tax credits, and as a result, we saw an increase in startup companies. This pandemic has given us the opportunity to branch out in this area; innovators can explore new methods of testing, or create a new app, or to research possible vaccines for COVID-19. Another area could be diversifying agriculture; growing our own food is essential since we are an island state and rely on much of our food being imported. Additionally, Hawaiʻi's goal of 100% renewable energy by 2045 puts us in the spotlight; we need to continue to move forward on this ambitious goal. If these types of companies are to be successful, it will take support from our government as well as from investors.

Quality of Life

There is virtually no traffic during this lockdown, when only essential workers are commuting to work. Studies in California have indicated that there are fewer traffic jams and less air pollution. In fact, the air in Los Angeles has had the longest period of good air days since 1995. People are working remotely from home and connecting via videoconferencing, emails, texts, phone calls, etc. Perhaps workers could be given the option to come to work for part of the week and work from home the remaining days. It would improve the workers' quality of life to not spend hours in traffic, and that could mean more time for themselves and/or for their families. Having employees work remotely can also impact traffic, with fewer cars on the road. It is an idea that I hope will be offered to employees.

Inequity and Inequality

This COVID-19 pandemic has clearly identified the inequity and inequality in our country today. Schools realize that many students have no access to Wi-Fi or technology or support from home, and sometimes, older children are expected to care for their younger siblings. Meanwhile students in higher income areas or in private schools continue to receive quality educational opportunities. The result could be a widening of the achievement gap when students return to school. Additionally, data shows that minorities are more at-risk to contract and to die from COVID-19; this is a problem that our government must address. Access to quality medical care is an issue for many low-income families or for those who cannot afford to take time off from work to go to the doctor. They are then more susceptible to long-term health conditions such as high blood pressure, diabetes, or asthma, issues that put them at-risk for COVID-19. Our government must address issues of income inequality and ensure that even those who cannot afford it will have access to affordable health insurance.

Family Time

Sheltering in place can mean more time for families to spend together. Photos on social media show parents and children playing board games, working on puzzles, building things, doing art projects, cooking, sewing, and having fun together. As I shared in my book, *Leading with Aloha: From the Pineapple Fields to the Principal's Office*, "Too often, we schedule our kids with multiple activities such as sports or dance or tutoring, leaving us exhausted and running from one activity to the next. This may mean rushing to get dinner started or picking up fast food if it's getting late. The kids are grouchy because they still have homework to do, and parents are annoyed with the kids for grumbling. Let's take a deep breath and really reflect on how we're spending our time." I hope families realize this gift of time they have been given and learn to prioritize what is really important.

Leadership

"When things are in turmoil, lead from the front. When things are going well, lead from the back." We are in turbulent times; no one could have predicted this pandemic and its impact on our world. We need strong leadership to get us through any crisis, leaders who are calm in the face of a crisis, who give us hope that we can get through this together, who are empathetic to our fears, who listen to advice from those who have more knowledge, and who answer questions honestly. As President Truman stated, "The buck stops here." Leaders know that they have the responsibility to make a decision and accept responsibility for that decision. Now, more than ever, we need strong leadership we can trust. We don't need a cheerleader in the back of the line; we need someone who will lead us through this turmoil.

We know that even after the lockdown is lifted, our behaviors will reflect the new habits that will become our new normal, and I hope that these months of uncertainty will lead to positive changes in our families, our schools, our communities, our state, our nation, and our world.

RACISM—WE MUST DO MORE IN SCHOOLS
June 4, 2020

I wasn't sure about whether I should write this blog post, but after I was done, I knew how important it had been to examine my own feelings and beliefs. It was humbling to realize that I had not done enough, nor had I discussed these kinds of issues with our staff when I was a principal or with my students when I was a teacher. I always preached about treating others with respect, but I didn't go deeper. I was concerned that I would cross the line of what was acceptable and what might be controversial.

I realize how wrong I was. We are sometimes so wrapped up in our own concerns that we downplay the feelings of others. Are we able to understand the challenges of those who are struggling? If so, what do we do to make things better for them as well as others who may be dealing with the same issues? Do we build positive relationships with others? Being aware of people's behaviors can give us cues to how they are feeling, and when we notice subtle changes, having a conversation can be just what is needed at that time. Empathetic leaders are good listeners and know that honest discussions can lead to the kind of trust that is essential to the organization.

I realize that even though Hawai'i is considered a melting pot of different cultures, it doesn't mean that we should shield our students from the difficult discussions about race.

In the midst of a pandemic, we suddenly are thrust into another crisis that has brought anger and strife into an already hurting world. The killing of a Black man by a white police officer in Minneapolis has forced us to closely examine our personal feelings. Do we feel anger or sadness or pity? Do we worry that someone we know may be placed in a similar situation? And we react differently. For some, this means going out in public to peacefully protest despite the health crisis we are presently experiencing. For others, it means sharing our angry thoughts and feelings on social media. For me, it meant examining my own actions when I was a school principal.

Our school was 99% military-impacted, and about 20% to 25% of our students identified as Black. During my tenure as principal from 2003–2018, we carefully reviewed data to ensure that all students were receiving an equitable education and the necessary services so they could be successful. We met regularly to share concerns about students who were having social, academic, or emotional challenges so we could collectively address their needs and share their progress. A good percentage were students of color, and I know we did our best to provide support for them. But was that enough? As I sit here and reflect, I realize that we could have and should have done more, not just for those struggling students but for *all* students. We should have taught them skills and strategies to be able to verbalize and to understand their own and other people's feelings and emotions. We should have done temperature checks to see whether our curriculum was making a difference for students. We should have paid better attention when students were struggling to understand the underlying reasons for their struggles. Just because racism was not evident at our school doesn't mean that it wasn't bubbling under the surface or that we shouldn't talk about it.

And that is the problem. We sweep difficult issues like racism to the side, or we water them down so we don't offend anyone, or we have discussions only when something like what happened in Minneapolis dominates the news. We learn about Martin Luther King Jr. or Ruby Bridges or Rosa Parks during Black History Month, but do we delve deeper into why they are an important part of our history or why we haven't made the progress we had hoped for? Do we ask our students to discuss issues of race at home, and do our students have the opportunity to interview their parents or grandparents or other family members about their experiences with racism? Do we let students research about other injustices in our history including against Native Americans, Native Hawaiians, Asian Americans, Hispanics, and others? When we teach social-emotional lessons to our little ones, do we talk about the color of one's skin and the beauty of diversity, or do we just talk about treating others with respect?

I remember reading *Black Like Me* by John Howard Griffin sometime in the early 1970s. It was not an assignment for school, so I never discussed the book with anyone. It was disturbing. I remember chatting with a young female teacher of color from New York. She shared that when she was a little girl, she saw her dad stopped by cops for being Black. Her parents emphasized that she had to be compliant if she was ever stopped by a police officer. She was a strong woman who spoke her mind, so her parents were probably very worried for her. I remember our meetings with parents of students who were Black and were having trouble controlling their anger when they were upset. These parents were very concerned and shared their fears that their child would face a difficult future if he/she was unable to control his/her anger. How do we teach our students to be strong and stick up for their rights when there is a real possibility of being hurt in the process because of the color of their skin?

I see posts from educators on social media about books to read and resources to use and how to prepare for those difficult discussions about racism when school resumes in the next few months, but it cannot be a few teachers in their classrooms. That discussion needs to involve all staff at a school as well as members of the community. We may feel that the topic of racism is not relevant for our students or our community because we have not experienced it. However, we cannot ignore the fact that the racial divide in our country has never been resolved, not since the Civil War ended or the riots and demonstrations of the 1960s. Racism simmers below the surface until it is suddenly thrust on us unexpectedly. Then we scramble to try to examine and address our personal feelings. By then, it is too late.

Being retired has provided me the opportunity to see issues more clearly. Our students today will be the leaders of tomorrow. We need them to learn about and to honestly discuss issues that will impact them, not just now, but in their future. We need teachers who are prepared to have frank and open discussions with their students. This will require professional development sessions on how to talk with kids about difficult issues. We need literature that addresses issues of racism or injustice. We need students to have opportunities to work collaboratively to address these sensitive issues and to offer a way forward for their school or their community. We need parents and community members to be more involved in addressing problems that are impacting our students and be part of the solution.

Empathy is the ability to understand the feelings of others. We may not have personally experienced racism and injustice, but if we have empathy, we know that the time to address these issues is long overdue. Let's make this a priority in schools.

Time to Examine Our Beliefs about Education
December 25, 2020

The longer the pandemic went on, the more I worried for our students, our teachers, and our school leaders. We read in news articles and on social media that many people don't believe that schools should change. Many are comfortable with what we've been doing for years—since the Industrial Age—and there has been no coordinated effort to discuss why we need to change.

What do we want for our students when they leave our school system? As a society, we need to have this discussion. That will determine what we need to focus on in order to provide a quality and relevant education for our students. Do we give students real-world experiences or is it all lectures, readings, and assignments? How do we prepare our students for their future? How do we ensure that they can be successful when they leave high school? How do we provide opportunities for students to explore what they are interested in rather than telling them what courses they need to take? There are so many questions and concerns that can and should be discussed with our stakeholders—educators, students, parents, and the community, including legislators. Without inclusive discussions, we may never change our educational system.

This is a blog post I feel most passionate about. It's a topic I've been thinking about throughout my educational career. In fact, I wrote about many of these topics in my blog, and I've shared them in this book. It is time for all of us to be part of the solution. We can make major changes to our educational system if we have the courage to examine our beliefs and to have difficult discussions.

These are challenging times as the COVID-19 pandemic continues to wreak havoc on our nation and our world. Yet we see those in essential positions continue their commitment as they work tirelessly during these challenging times. That is true of our educators; learning how to adapt during a pandemic was never a part of the college coursework to becoming a teacher. I applaud my fellow educators for continuing to be their best for their students. Yet I feel the urgency to have meaningful discussions about our schools and our educational systems. There is so much about our schools that needs to be changed, and this pandemic and its impact on education can be the impetus for discussions.

When I was a principal, I sometimes faced difficult decisions between toeing the line and listening to my gut feelings about what was best for our school, our students, and our teachers. I wanted our staff to think outside of the box and to be innovative. Yet, I knew that as the principal, I needed to be aware of the expectations of our schools and regulations that needed to be adhered to. How do we balance the two when they were sometimes not in sync?

Now that schools have had to change due to the pandemic and

safety issues related to being back in school, the time is ripe to discuss how to make schools more relevant. As a principal, I would often think about different scenarios and ponder how we might change the way we've always done education:

- Those of us in education see firsthand the correlation between socioeconomic status and student achievement. Societal factors have a huge impact on some of our most needy students, and expecting them to be able to focus on school when their basic needs are not met is unrealistic. We know that given time and a caring staff, schools can have a positive impact on disadvantaged students. We know that school can be the one constant in a child's life, the one safe place where family problems can be forgotten for a few hours. How do we address the socioeconomic gap and its impact on education so that *all* students have equal opportunities to be successful?
- We know that every student is different and that when they begin school, they do not start at the same starting line; in fact, some students are far behind other students when they first enter kindergarten, but we expect them to be at the same place at the end of the year. Think of it as a running race; can we reasonably expect someone to start half a lap behind and finish at the same time as others who started with a big lead? How should we be measuring progress in school?
- During this pandemic, teachers shared how much they learned and how they collaborated with colleagues to create classrooms where social-emotional learning was as important as academics. If we agree that positive relationships between students and with their teachers can make a difference, how can we use that knowledge to positively impact teaching and learning?
- Seat time and good grades are not necessarily an indication

of learning. Too often, learning in school is merely memorizing and regurgitating information. Real learning means applying skills or facts to delve deeper, to make sense of information, and the application to new situations. It may mean that students get feedback, then revise their work before submitting it for credit. How do we change our reporting system to tell the story of real learning that has lasting impact on a student?

- Too often, school is teacher-directed. It is the teacher in the classroom who determines what to teach, when to teach it, and what is the evidence of learning. Students are often passive learners as opposed to being passionate, self-directed learners whose curiosity about a subject drives their own learning. How can we ensure that our student learners have an opportunity to create their own learning that is meaningful and impactful to them?
- This pandemic provided evidence that face-to-face learning is not the only option for K–12 schools. Technology is an equalizer; students can learn just as well through blended and/or virtual learning; in fact, some students thrived in this environment. How will schools reconfigure how they provide teaching and learning now that options other than face-to-face have shown to be successful?
- The public judges schools based on standardized test scores, and schools feel the pressure of ensuring that their students are prepared for this once-a-year, high-stakes testing. Teachers may be evaluated based on the scores of their students. Unfortunately, the reports that schools receive are rarely useful. Teachers have no way of examining their student responses to see what kinds of errors were made. While we understand that the public needs to know that our schools are educating our students to be contributing citizens of their community, is there a more reliable, less expensive, and less time-consuming way to rate our schools

besides high-stakes testing?
- One of the frustrations I had as a principal was not having sufficient funding for our students to experience a well-rounded education that included music, physical education, visual arts, drama, STEM, etc. Our teachers needed support, too—dedicated mentors for new teachers, instructional coaches, technology coaches, etc. This pandemic showed the dedication of our teachers to plug away despite the challenges they faced. While we understand the fiscal challenges our states are facing, the question of funding for schools will not go away. If our children are our priority, shouldn't our schools be adequately funded?

Soon, we will have a new secretary of education. These discussions, at the national, state, and district levels, are long overdue. Let's hope we can finally work to improve our systems so that all students, no matter where they live, can have access to a quality education.

What Does the Future Hold for Education?
Reflective Questions

- What are the biggest hurdles educators face, and what can we do about it?
- How do challenges in education impact the future of our communities?
- What are some problems that your school faces? How can you involve the school community in addressing these problems?
- What are changes you would recommend for our schools? Why are these important to you, and what can you do about it?
- How do we involve student voice when we have discussions about educational reform? Why is student voice important?

- How can we ensure that schools have sufficient resources to provide an equitable and quality education for their students?
- How can we involve the community as part of the solution to reform education?
- Jack Welch shares, "Change before you have to." What does this mean for teachers, for schools, and for the educational system? What changes should be made now? Why?

NOTES

Afterword

LOOKING AHEAD

During my tenure as principal, I was able to visit a few other schools in Hawaiʻi and Las Vegas to discuss educational issues with their staff or school leaders. Additionally, in 2014, I was part of a Department of Education team that visited school districts in Los Angeles, Las Vegas, and Edmonton to learn about school empowerment. Also, our students were able to share what they were learning with legislative and military leaders who visited our school. That, I feel, was the best way to show these leaders how schools were changing to be more student-centered and community-based. As I look back on my principalship, I realize how fortunate I was to have these opportunities.

Our schools have much to share. Unfortunately, too often, there just isn't the time or commitment that allows teachers and principals to visit other schools to observe, question, discuss, network, and reflect on ways to improve. There are so many other teaching and leading responsibilities, and connecting and learning from other educators is often not a priority.

We, in Hawaiʻi, have another problem. I remember reading Governor John Burns's words, "subtle inferiority of the spirit," or the feeling in Hawaiʻi that we are not as good as our mainland counterparts. I think that carries over to our educational system here in our state. When I encourage teachers to share their stories and what they are doing, so many of them tell me, "But I'm not doing anything special." Contrary to that idea, however, schools in Hawaiʻi are doing great things. Ted Dintersmith, author of *What School Could Be*,[16] shares about his visit to Hawai'i schools in this way: "These visits were like watching the finale of the Fourth of July fireworks celebration—one spectacular burst of innovation after another." One reason why I loved my job as a principal was that I could document and share exciting teaching and learning that was going on in our classrooms and at our schools, not just with our school community, but with the larger educational community on social media.

Educator reformer John Dewey said, "Education is not preparation for life; education is life itself." Yet we often equate the word "education" with schools rather than seeing education as a lifelong goal that we should all strive for. Throughout my career as an educator and even after retiring, I aim to be, as our son Justin stated in the foreword to this book, a student of education—to learn more, to do more, to be more. I have learned from others and with others, sharing opinions, ideas, successes, and challenges. I read books, articles, and blogs; engage in conversations in-person and virtually; and reflect via my blog.

When I began blogging in 2012, I had no idea what to expect. When I look back, I can see my growth and confidence, not only as a writer, but also as an educator. Today, I realize what an opportunity I have had to share my thoughts and opinions with the public. Even though I am retired, I will continue to advocate for students, educators, and our schools because there are still so many unresolved issues that impact education in our country and in our state. We cannot get complacent. ♥

References

1. "You Know What Really 'Sucks' about School?" by Peter DeWitt https://www.edweek.org/education/opinion-you-know-what-really-sucks-about-school/2015/08

2. "What Holds Us Back From Focusing on School Climate?" by Peter DeWitt https://www.edweek.org/education/opinion-what-holds-us-back-from-focusing-on-school-climate/2015/08

3. cainesarcade.com

4. "Marshmallow Challenge" https://youtu.be/RtQr9w2pL74

5. "The Little Boy" by Helen Buckley http://www.ndlcpreschool.com/wp-content/uploads/2013/07/THE-LITTLE-BOY.pdf

6. "Do schools kill creativity" by Sir Ken Robinson https://www.ted.com/talks/sir_ken_robinson_do_schools_kill_creativity

7. *Life's Literacy Lessons* https://www.stenhouse.com/content/lifes-literacy-lessons

8. "The Reading Wars" https://www.theatlantic.com/magazine/archive/1997/11/the-reading-wars/376990/

9. "The Goal of Phonics Instruction is to Get Readers Not to Use Phonics When Reading" https://therobbreviewblog.com/uncategorized/get-readers-not-to-use-phonics-when-reading/

10. "8 Characteristics Of A Great Teacher" https://www.teach

thought.com/pedagogy/8-characteristics-of-a-great-teacher/

11. "What teaching is and isn't" https://www.washingtonpost.com/news/answer-sheet/wp/2014/05/05/what-teaching-is-and-isnt-or-teachingis/

12. "Helping Military Children Feel 'At Ease'" https://www.naesp.org/resource/helping-military-children-feel-at-ease/

13. "Daniel K. Inouye Elementary School—Our $33.2 Million Project!" http://hkesfollowourprogress.blogspot.com/

14. "Systematic Approach to Building 21st Century Schools: Experiences in the Aloha State" https://eric.ed.gov/?id=EJ967564

15. "UH effort aims to grow pool of teachers in isles" https://www.staradvertiser.com/2017/09/19/hawaii-news/uh-effort-aims-to-grow-pool-of-teachers-in-isles?/

16. *What School Could Be* by Ted Dintersmith (page 207)

About the Author

Jan Iwase, a lifelong resident of Hawaiʻi, grew up in a pineapple plantation village on the island of Oʻahu and graduated from the University of Hawaiʻi at Mānoa. In 2002, after teaching in the Head Start program and in the state Department of Education (DOE), she was named principal of Hale Kula Elementary School, later renamed the Daniel K. Inouye Elementary School. She was chosen as the DOE's Central District Elementary Principal of the Year in 2013 and was nominated for the Masayuki Tokioka Excellence in School Leadership award in 2016. Jan retired as principal in 2018 after 45 years as an educator and today lives in Mililani with her husband, Randy. She is the mother of three sons, Justin, Jarand and Jordan.

In 2019, Jan published *Leading with Aloha: From the Pineapple Fields to the Principal's Office*. This is her second book.